INTELLECTUAL PROPERTY STRATEGY

JOHN PALFREY

D0124480

The MIT Press | Cambridge, Massachusetts | London, England

This book was set in Chaparral Pro by the MIT Press. Printed and bound in the United States of America.

Library of Congress Cataloging-in-Publication Data

Palfrey, John G.
Intellectual property strategy / John Palfrey.
    p.   cm.
Includes bibliographical references and index.
ISBN 978-0-262-51679-2 (pbk. : alk. paper)
1. Intellectual property—Management. I. Title.
HD53.P35   2011
658.15'2—dc22

                                                              2011011493

10   9   8   7   6   5

For Terry Fisher, whose every idea makes perfect sense immediately

CONTENTS

Available online (at http://mitpress.mit.edu/ipstrategy):

Case Studies

SERIES FOREWORD

The MIT Press Essential Knowledge series presents short, accessible books on need-to-know subjects in a variety of fields. Written by leading thinkers, Essential Knowledge volumes deliver concise, expert overviews of topics ranging from the cultural and historical to the scientific and technical. In our information age, opinion, rationalization, and superficial descriptions are readily available. Much harder to come by are the principled understanding and foundational knowledge needed to inform our opinions and decisions. This series of beautifully produced, pocket-sized, soft-cover books provides in-depth, authoritative material on topics of current interest in a form accessible to nonexperts. Instead of condensed versions of specialist texts, these books synthesize anew important subjects for a knowledgeable audience. For those who seek to enter a subject via its fundamentals, Essential Knowledge volumes deliver the understanding and insight needed to navigate a complex world.

Bruce Tidor
Professor of Biological Engineering and Computer Science
Massachusetts Institute of Technology

I have written this book in two related, yet distinct, formats. As a conventional matter, this book might be read in the printed form that you now hold in your hands. This is, purposely, a short book, designed to give you a primer on intellectual property strategy in no more time that it takes to fly, say, from New York to London or Boston to Los Angeles, if you were to read it cover-to-cover in a single sitting.

As an experimental matter, I've also written the book, as well as a series of companion case studies and related material, to be read in a purely digital format. The idea behind this digital version is to experiment with whether a reader might benefit from a presentation of these ideas that is at once both linear and nonlinear. While you can make your way through the text just as you might the conventional, printed version (albeit on a screen), you are offered a series of places where you might take a deeper dive into one or more topics that especially interest you.

These potential diversions, built into the digital version of the book, take the form of a series of case studies and short videos. These supplements are designed to enable you to go deeper on many of the big themes developed in the conventional form of the book. Via links within the text, you will find connections to case studies on a range of topics. For instance, these cases take up follow-on biologics, an important form of innovation in the market for lifesaving drugs internationally; the practice of licensing trademarks in the collegiate market; university technology commercialization; open innovation, in particular the InnoCentive model; the story of Starbucks and its attempts to trademark coffee from Africa; and the licensing opportunities seized by major museums, such as the Louvre in France.

These brief cases also include links to the open web. My hope is that you might at some point, after such a detour, return to the book, rather than allowing yourself to be pulled into the deeper web. Even if you don't return to the book, that is a risk I consider worth taking. There is, after all, more to be said on the topic of intellectual property strategy than I've included in either version of this book.

The videos are interviews that I have recorded with experts in the field of intellectual property. You can watch these videos in full, via the iPad application or on YouTube. You will also find pointers to snippets from the videos embedded in the text of the digital version of the book in places where I encourage you to take a detour to hear from someone other than me, the primary author.

Last, and most important in a way, I hope that you will talk back: to challenge the ideas I've put forward here in this book, online and in public, to help build our common understanding of the world of ideas, knowledge, and innovation in today's global marketplace. It is through this kind of public exchange that we can together grow smarter about intellectual property.

ACKNOWLEDGMENTS

I owe thanks to a great team of collaborators. June Casey, my colleague at Harvard Law School, has proven to me, yet again, how important truly great librarians are, especially in a digital era. June provided substantive and editorial advice on both the main text and the online materials, including the case studies, videos, and user interface. She also managed and supported an able group of law students who have also contributed mightily to this project. In partnership with June, David Jacobs researched and drafted most of the case studies that accompany this volume. Daniel Doktori researched and drafted the case on university technology licensing. Andrew Breidenbach provided valuable research assistance for the primary text of the book. My colleagues at the Berkman Center for Internet & Society at Harvard University have provided deep inspiration. Dean Martha Minow, Terry Fisher, Urs Gasser, Lawrence Lessig, Phil Malone, and Jonathan Zittrain have been generous with their ideas. Margy Avery and her team at the MIT Press, as well as the group of blind peer reviewers that she assembled, have been a pleasure to work with. My family, as ever, has been patient and supportive through yet another book project that cut into my time on the playground and Little League diamond.

INTRODUCTION

The Self-Limiting Myth of the Sword and the Shield

Copyrights: Your Sword and Your Shield.

—S&E Entertainment–Music Publishing, October 1, 2009

The sword and shield of patent protection: *Nokia v. Apple/ Apple v. Nokia*.

—Chris F. Lonegro, Ober Kaler law firm, February 2, 2010

In the first instance, intellectual property rights in patent, trademark or copyright are used as a sword. . . . [In other cases, l]itigation becomes a shield.

—Intellect Law Group, 2010

[Intervention by a competition authority is justified w]hen a patent owner uses his patent rights not only as a shield to protect his invention, but as a sword to eviscerate competition unfairly.

—*Atari Games Corp. v. Nintendo*, 897 F.2d 1572 (Fed. Cir. 1990)

In conventional wisdom, intellectual property strategy is about the sword and the shield. As a sword, intellectual property can be used to attack a competitor who seeks to exploit some aspect of your intellectual property in a way that violates your rights. As a shield, intellectual property can help you to stave off the attacks of your competitors. That's still true—but only to an extent. This outdated metaphor, invoking the battlefield, suggests that you should control and exploit your intellectual property to the greatest extent allowed by law in every instance, no matter the context and no matter who you are. This theory no longer describes the best approach for most institutions, much of the time.

In this book, I argue that intellectual property should first evoke images of the boardroom and its deal-making table—and only later the courtroom, if things go terribly wrong, but as a last resort. The people who benefit the most from these disputes ending up in court are the lawyers who make their living on the fees generated in these disputes, which routinely run into the millions or tens of millions of dollars. As someone responsible for your organization—whether a business or nonprofit, a government agency or university—you are much less likely to benefit from an exclusive sword-and-shield strategy with respect to your intellectual property than is your lawyer.

If you are like many managers, you probably don't pay much attention to your organization's intellectual property.

This book, a short briefing intended for an audience of senior managers, is designed to change that. I contend that intellectual property strategy deserves greater attention from both senior managers of corporations and administrators of nonprofits like universities in a wide range of fields. This argument is not only relevant to those who run high-tech, for-profit organizations. I claim that the traditional way of thinking about intellectual property within the organization will have a negative and limiting impact, leading to shortsighted decisions if you don't look beyond it. Flexibility and creativity are essential to a profitable long-term intellectual property strategy. Strategies grounded in openness and connectedness to others (in technical terms, "interoperability") can offer surprising benefits to those who are willing to experiment with new approaches.

You should instead think of intellectual property as a flexible asset class that can help your organization in a broad range of ways. In formulating your overall strategy, you should give special consideration to strategies of openness rather than exclusion, especially in the information context. This advice holds true regardless of the type of institution you are leading, whether a for- or nonprofit, whether you are well established or a start-up.

At the broadest level, intellectual property is a way of describing what the people in your organization know and are capable of doing. It's the collected knowledge, work product,

Strategies grounded in openness and connectedness to others (in technical terms, "interoperability") can offer surprising benefits to those who are willing to experiment with new approaches.

and skill set of all the people who make up your team. Even the know-how of your staff at large explicitly has value. Sometimes an intellectual property-related transaction requires the hiring of staff members who know how to implement the intellectual property, whether as part of a licensing deal, merger, or acquisition, or in a bankruptcy setting. Those who think about "knowledge management" as part of the organization's overall strategy will get this concept intuitively.

At the same time, intellectual property is also an essential, flexible asset class that can help you accomplish a range of goals, from accessing new markets to improving existing products to generating new revenue streams. By "flexible," I mean that intellectual property can be more than just a line item on the balance sheet; it can be used in a wide range of ways to help achieve your organization's mission in short-, medium-, and long-term ways. What I mean by "asset class" is that intellectual property is an important set of resources available to any senior manager as you seek to achieve your overall mission, which has intrinsic value that can be worked into a balance sheet.

In many organizations, intellectual property should be viewed as a key strategic class of assets. The global intellectual property licensing market for trademarks and copyrights alone tops one hundred billion dollars per year. Organizations headquartered in the United States and Canada earn nearly seventy billion dollars of that total annual revenue. The licensing of patents adds billions more.[1] If that market size alone doesn't get your attention, consider the fact that intellectual property makes up 40 percent of the net asset value of all corporations in the United States.[2] In a cultural institution, think of the value—which can also reach the millions or billions of dollars—of the collections you hold. For any organization, the brand value in your name and logo may be extraordinarily worthwhile in its own right.

The primary message in this book is simple: you need to think broadly and creatively about how you invest in your organization's intellectual property asset base, and how you use it. As you might guess, that's much easier said than done. Whether or not your organization is already an active participant in the emerging marketplace of ideas and skills, there are opportunities to increase your licensing of intellectual property to achieve your business goals. A licensing strategy might involve looking at the valuation of your intellectual property (IP) portfolio in a new way. This strategy might involve licensing what you already have in your IP portfolio. It might mean acquiring more IP one way or another. Or it might mean giving away some of your rights for long-term strategic reasons.

The simple argument that runs through this book is that you should consider each of these approaches as part of your tool kit. The secondary and subtler assertion is that you should favor strategies of relative openness where they can offer greater long-term benefits than strategies of exclusion. Regardless of the approach you choose in any given situation, it's increasingly important to get your intellectual property strategy right—and focus on its evolution, in a fast-changing marketplace—to be competitive in a global knowledge economy.

Key Strategic Moves in Intellectual Property

There are many crucial strategic moves beyond the concepts of the sword and the shield that you can make using intellectual property. First, there is a wide range of ways that you can acquire intellectual property in the first place. When you innovate, whether in a for- or nonprofit setting, you are almost certainly establishing some form of intellectual property rights. You can also obtain rights by licensing intellectual property from someone else in a way that will help you to grow your business or expand your margins. It might mean entering into a joint development agreement to pool your intellectual property with others to create something innovative together. You might even get your customers to contribute intellectual property to you as they use your products or services. In many cases, customers will generously contribute this intellectual property to you for free. You should open yourself up to the opportunity to receive their contributions.

Second, there's a broader range of things you can do with your intellectual property once you've established these rights. At the most basic level, you can exercise your rights to their fullest extent to exclude others from using your intellectual property. I call that strategy "full exclusion." That's the classic approach, and it sometimes makes good sense for an organization. But it might sometimes pay off handsomely for you to license, sell, or give away certain rights, while retaining others for yourself. You might also offer it to others to use on a limited basis, or "limited exclusion." Finally, you might offer it up for anyone to use for any purpose, or "open access," in ways that may help you gain a market share or fulfill your organization's mission. Each of these potential strategies could constitute part of your organization's overall intellectual property strategy. Which of these strategies you apply in a given situation will depend on a host of factors.

The best intellectual property strategy will be flexible. A flexible strategic approach will prompt you to ask hard, context-specific questions about which approach along this spectrum makes sense for any given type of intellectual property at a given time. The most innovative organizations employ multiple types of uses, depending on the situation. Advanced intellectual property licensing strategies can also help build market share, improve the quality or attractiveness of existing products, develop productive relationships with your customers, and grow your organization and industry or field as a whole. Intellectual property can help build a thriving business or nonprofit ecosystem from which many players as well as consumers or patrons stand to benefit.

The most vibrant ecosystems may prove to be those in which consumers don't just "consume" products but in fact volunteer their services to help innovate with and alongside organizations, as we've seen in parts of the software and Web 2.0 industries. This shift is easiest to see in the context of nonprofits, such as universities, libraries, and museums. But it can be just as true in the business context, especially in information technology (IT) and content-related sectors. It's true, too, in the context of design, fashion, biotechnology, and a range of other unexpected domains.

Just as the rewards for getting and using your intellectual property today are higher, the risks involved in this aspect of business are also higher than they were just a few decades ago. The intellectual property business is "high beta"—the term that investors use to describe an asset that offers high risk and high reward, unlike, say, cash reserves. The costs of licensing someone else's intellectual property can be extremely high; the costs of not licensing and using it anyway can be even higher.

On the bright side, if you can become an entity that licenses intellectual property to others—a "licensor," in legalese—you can generate attractive rates of return on your investment. Intellectual property licensing is such a big business in part because it can generate so much free cash flow. It's also a big deal because it can help both parties to grow. And it's on many managers' minds because the downside of getting it wrong in the first place can be enormous.

Intellectual Property Matters to Your Organization (Yes, Even Yours)

You might think, off the bat, that intellectual property is just a matter of concern to big, established for-profit companies in fields like biotech, software, or publishing that have large licensing operations. It is certainly crucial to those firms. But as the global knowledge economy grows each year, the importance of intellectual property strategy also grows for nonprofit organizations such as universities, libraries, museums, public media producers, and a broad range of cultural heritage institutions.

Intellectual property can mean many different things to different kinds of organizations. That makes it a broad topic for a short book. Intellectual property generally takes the form of rights that vest in creators of innovative ideas, expressions, processes, and brands. These rights are established by law, and granted to people or organizations through four primary types of interests: patents (for ideas and methods, which in time are made public), copyrights (for expressive works), trademarks (for protecting and eliminating confusion with respect to brands), and trade secrets (for methods of doing things that are not made public).[3]

Pretty much every organization has an intellectual property portfolio of some kind and value, whether or not the organization realizes it as such. As a result, virtually every organization needs an intellectual property strategy, even if it's a simple one. The easiest way to see this point is that every organization has a brand that describes it to the outside world, which is itself an important form of intellectual property. That's true of a fancy university like MIT or Ole Miss in the United States, Oxford in England, or Keio in Japan. Think of all the sweatshirts that a big collegiate sports program sells for major public institutions like the University of Nebraska or the University of North Carolina. It's true, too, of institutions such as the Smithsonian, the Tate, or the Hermitage. And it is certainly true of a business of any kind.

There's a second, more subtle point that draws most organizations into the intellectual property field as well. We are increasingly operating in an economy that revolves around the production and management of information rather than physical production. The more that an organization is involved in managing information, the more likely the firm is to be operating in the realm of intellectual property, as opposed to physical property, in a variety of respects.

Consider the case of Triumvirate Environmental, a leading company in the US hazardous waste business. John McQuillan, the CEO of Triumvirate Environmental, once told me, "I'm not in the environment business. I'm in the information business."[4]

Yes, it's true that Triumvirate Environmental is a company that makes most of its money in a literal sense by charging its consumers for treating hazardous waste and carrying it away in their signature green trucks to a safe place. On another level, though, what McQuillan is really doing for his clients is providing and managing the information about this waste along with the fact that it was properly handled. This information is of great importance to regulators, business partners, and the public. This information itself is intellectual property. If, like McQuillan's Triumvirate Environmental, you're really in the "information" business on any level, you need an intellectual property strategy.

Like the global information economy at large, the field of intellectual property is emerging quickly. It is very much in flux, which is a key reason why a flexible strategy is so critical. Things are changing in terms of everyday practice; "social norms," or the way in which people think about and act with respect to intellectual property; and the law itself, especially when one takes a worldwide view. With every passing year, the marketplace for intellectual property becomes ever-more global. Major markets, like China and India, are fast becoming intellectual property creators rather than just net intellectual property consumers (or worse, pirates). As the world shifts away from an industrial economy to a knowledge economy, intellectual property is increasingly becoming a coin of the global business realm.

But it's much more complex than other asset classes. Depending on the kind of organization that you run, intellectual property might seem more like a minefield, commons, and/or public relations tinderbox. These multiple facets of intellectual property call for careful, proactive management, which is one of the key premises of this book.

No matter what industry you are in, you need to think about intellectual property more flexibly and expansively than your predecessors once did. The law is changing, and sometimes rapidly, on an international basis. That's true whether you are talking about copyrights, patents, or trademarks. The biggest changes are coming in terms of how business leaders are thinking about intellectual property in strategic terms. Strategy in this area is dramatically different today than it was even a decade or two ago. This book is designed to suggest ways to establish an intellectual property strategy that will be up to date for today's global information economy and also endure the inevitable changes of tomorrow.

Intellectual Property Strategy presents the state of the art in thinking on intellectual property to CEOs, senior managers, and those aspiring to lead any type of organization. The twin goals of this book are to point to the areas of greatest importance in this fast-moving field and offer practical insights to senior managers on how to create a strategy to enable an organization to address the challenges and opportunities that these areas hold.

In full disclosure, along the way I intend to nudge you toward exploring strategies of openness on the basis of their long-term business promise as well as the relationship between your intellectual property strategy and your brand. In doing so, I refer, one way or another, to each of the four essential areas of intellectual property—patent, copyright, trademark, and trade secret—from the perspectives of a range of types of organizations.

This book is built around four recommendations. I suggest that regardless of the type of organization you run, you should:

1. Consider intellectual property to be an asset class (rather than solely as a sword and a shield). You need first to establish this asset class, understand its near- and long-term value, then manage it, and find ways to use it to expand the range of opportunities to achieve your core mission, whether that is profitability for your firm or a broadly public-interested outcome.

2. Be open to what your customers, competitors, and others can offer you in terms of intellectual property. Your most important intellectual property might come from unlikely sources. And in many instances, your organization is situated in an intellectual property ecosystem that can support the growth and profitability of multiple participants if the ecosystem itself thrives in a cooperative environment.

3. Build from the premise that intellectual property is most valuable insofar as it creates freedom of action for your organization rather than serving as an offensive weapon against others. As a related concept, you should understand the extent to which your brand value is intertwined with intellectual property rights in ways that you can't disentangle.

4. Establish a strategy that enables you to be creative and flexible in what you do with your intellectual property—by thinking beyond the sword and the shield. In so doing, you should be sure to consider strategies—more than you have in the past—that harness the power of greater openness and interoperability as among your key options.

If you ignore, neglect, or fail to manage your intellectual property, you are probably running unnecessary risks as an organization. And you are almost certainly missing opportunities. That's increasingly true in many industries as the knowledge economy grows. By taking the four basic steps outlined in this book, you can mitigate these risks. At the same time, you can lead your organization to greater success, whether you define that as higher profits, a stronger balance sheet, better products, closer relationships with your customers and business partners over time, or more visitors to your institution or Web site. You will be contributing to the development of a knowledge-based ecosystem from which your organization will stand to benefit over the long term. All the while, you will be positioning your organization for success in the global information economy.

WHY INTELLECTUAL PROPERTY MATTERS

Intellectual property is not a legal backwater best left by CEOs to their lawyers at a big outside law firm. It is at the core of what drives businesses and many other types of organizations forward. Every institution holds intellectual property of varying degrees of importance to the fulfillment of its mission. It's what an organization's community knows in the aggregate and what its people can do. Intellectual property is often a key driver of new business lines. It can also be a driver of revenues, both directly and indirectly, in the form of free cash flow. And it can be a creative way to build new connections to your customers, patrons, business partners, and prospects.

Two recent stories—each from a different field of business, and both true—illustrate why you should care about your intellectual property strategy.

The Smartphone

Let's say you want to develop a new smartphone to compete with Apple's blockbuster iPhone. You know, off the bat, that there are thousands of patents standing between you and the launch of your new smartphone. In intellectual property lawyer speak, you may hear someone tell you that there are thousands of patents that "read" on the phone you are proposing to build.

Samsung had such a plan in mind a few years ago. It set about to develop a new, competitive smartphone to take back some of the market share claimed by the likes of Apple. But as Samsung found, a semiconductor company called InterDigital, based in King of Prussia, Pennsylvania, had a series of patents based on innovations over several decades. After a long-running and distracting patent-infringement fight, in January 2009, Samsung agreed to pay InterDigital $400 million over four years. Nokia was already on the hook for a $253 million payment to Inter-Digital. (Set aside for the moment the hard problem of whether InterDigital's work constituted real innovation or the operations of a "patent troll," also known as "non-practicing entities"—a method of merely holding up companies from obtaining licenses—as some allege.)

So why wasn't this a problem for Apple, the maker of the iPhone?[1] Or for Research in Motion (RIM), which makes the BlackBerry? Neither of these giants of the smartphone industry ran into this same trouble in court, at least on this score. The reason is that they both had negotiated licenses up front with InterDigital. The InterDigital intellectual property was already part of their portfolio—their "bundle of rights"—when they went to market with their product.[2]

Perhaps Samsung will end up passing Apple and RIM in the smartphone business. (They have some promising smartphones on the market that run Google's Android system, which is fast gaining a market share as of 2011.) And perhaps the InterDigital licensing matter had little to do with the outcome, in which Apple and RIM have been thriving, and Samsung has struggled to succeed in the US market. No matter what, Samsung lost time, focus, and money as a result of getting tangled with InterDigital.

The lesson: like it or not, the intellectual property that other organizations have amassed matters a great deal in terms of enabling you to pursue your emerging business goals. Like it or not, you have to accept that the rights of other organizations will set the playing field—and may affect the ultimate outcome of the game.

As in the case of Apple and RIM, it will pay off to do your homework first and initiate your business plan grounded in a keen assessment of the risks that lie around you in the intellectual property ecosystem. You may decide to run certain risks and plow ahead as planned, or you may pause to consider alternate means of proceeding. At a minimum, your strong understanding of the intellectual property landscape will surely help to decide how much to invest in the business line, how to assess its prospects, and the range of possible outcomes.

The Lovable Character

The Children's Television Workshop (CTW) launched *Sesame Street* in 1969. In developing the concept, it consulted pediatricians, psychologists, and educators of many stripes. It came up with a hit television series. Along the way, it dreamed up a series of characters to teach children through educational television. Through the characters and the creativity of the programming, the CTW managed to develop a strong connection with the kids who tuned in to its shows.

One of the characters, Elmo, struck a particular chord with children. Elmo is usually up to something interesting—though tame, of course—and carries it out in a sweet, bumbling manner. It's not clear if Elmo is a boy or girl. Young children just learning to speak and interact with the world—ages two or three, especially—relate to Elmo in an uncanny way. It is hard to describe the connection that kids feel toward Elmo. But as many parents know, it can be extremely strong.

The CTW was founded to create educational television shows, not to manufacture products. It's also a nonprofit. But that has not stopped it from making a great deal of money from the relationship that Elmo has with fans. For more than a decade, the CTW has been licensing certain trademark rights and copyrights that it holds in Elmo—along with friends Big Bird, Grover, and others—to for-profit organizations. It has set out to create and exploit a licensing market for their characters not just in the United States but also around the world. And they've been exceptionally successful in this regard.

Now picture yourself, as a parent, walking down the juice aisle in the supermarket. Your three-year-old is in the child seat of the shopping cart. You reach for the lowest-priced apple juice, and just then, your child notices Elmo on a smaller, pricier bottle. After a brief, intense negotiation, you switch apple juices. You end up buying the more expensive bottle. You pay more for less in the way of apple juice, but avoid a major public battle with your little one. The net effect of this everyday story is that millions of dollars flow to the CTW and higher profits accrue to the manufacturers that take out a license to use Elmo's image on consumer-facing food products.

There's another benefit that is important to mention at this stage. It's possible that the CTW would have gone down the road of licensing the use of its characters purely for the money. But it's gotten another benefit from this strategy: much greater reach for its characters and ideas. Through these deals, other people *pay* the CTW for the right to spread the word about its characters. So long as the CTW makes good choices about its partnerships, the net effect of licensing is not just money but also greater value in the brand itself (up to a point) and more kids coming back to watch the programs that feature the characters. A sound licensing strategy drives both parts of the CTW's double bottom line.

One might tell a similar story about Dora the Explorer, owned by Viacom, the parent of Nickelodeon and Nick Jr., because the tweens and teens segment is particularly hot today. *Disney's High School Musical*, for instance, is considered an especially desirable brand to license. Or Disney's hit princess characters—based, by the way, not on characters that Disney's on-staff "creatives" dreamed up but instead on popular stories long in the public domain, such as *Snow White* and *Beauty and the Beast*. Both Viacom and Disney are profiting handsomely from the sales of their hit characters and entertainment properties. While Viacom doesn't have the same public-interested mission that the CTW does, the effective licensing of Dora materials contributes to the likelihood that a child will visit Dora's Web site or look for her shows in the on-demand section of their cable offerings, which drives a virtuous cycle.

These stories each make a slightly different point about the importance of intellectual property to your organization. The first is about the significance of obtaining and using patent rights, with a proactive rather than reactive mind-set. It's clear that one would rather be Apple or InterDigital than Samsung or Nokia. The second narrative, about trademark and copyright interests, demonstrates how the educators and producers behind *Sesame Street* have created an extraordinary public service enterprise, and have additionally fueled it with character-related, cash-producing marketing as well as free exposure for their brands. In each of these cases, smart intellectual property strategy has led to big returns for the organizations that have leveraged the intangible but highly valuable knowledge-based assets of their organizations.

What Is Intellectual Property, Exactly?

What can you protect through intellectual property rights? Generally, original ideas, expressive works, and the words and images (and even sounds and colors) that describe brands can be protected through intellectual property systems. For example, a novel method of manufacturing something can be patented through the US Patent and Trademark Office and its counterparts around the world. The process often takes several years to obtain an issued patent, but you can frequently produce benefits for your organization even through the act of filing a patent application. (In some cases, business methods can be patented too, though current trends in the law point toward greater and greater difficulty in patenting such processes.)[3] When you come up with a new logo or brand for your service or product, you can register that "mark"—a trademark or service mark—at the state and federal levels in the United States as well as other jurisdictions around the world where you plan to do business. The same goes for copyrighting a new song, book, movie script, or the like.

It is worth pausing for a moment to acknowledge that we're in the midst of a major, multiyear political dispute about intellectual property. Though not the primary topic of this book, there's a vibrant discussion in the United States and other countries about whether intellectual property rights have grown too much over the past two hundred years. For instance, the extension of the copyright term in 1998—the Sonny Bono Copyright Term Extension Act tacked on twenty years to the length of time that a copyright holder has to enjoy their exclusive rights, now for a period measured by their lifetime plus seventy years— gave rise to a US Supreme Court challenge. The challengers, led by law professor Lawrence Lessig, made a forceful argument against copyright term extension, but came up short by a vote of seven to two. The efforts of the Recording Industry Association of America to enforce the copyright interests of its members, the music recording labels, has prompted a backlash among customers and a movement called "Free Culture" on college campuses. The debates over patent reform are just as robust. The largest of the questions are: How and when do intellectual property rights inhibit or stimulate innovation, and how can we optimize the system from a public policy vantage point? These are important political discussions, and it would be smart to be aware of and perhaps participate in them as they develop further. (A few of the books, blogs, and other Web sites in the reading list at the end of this book cover these debates along with the related intellectual property issues. I say a bit more on this front in chapter 9.)[4]

For my purposes here, let's take the intellectual property regime as it is.[5] My premise is to consider together what you might do, as a company, within the legal and business framework of intellectual property as it exists today. In the best intellectual property strategies, you will anticipate and benefit from future trends as well.

The process of acquiring intellectual property begins with an analysis of how best to go about it. Before you can enter a new market or launch a new product, not only do you need to have a thorough knowledge of your business ecosystem; you also have to come up with the human and financial capital to make it successful. You hire a team and convince someone—your board, a bank, a customer, or an angel investor—to put up the capital that you know is needed to fund the necessary work. Now is also the right time, at the beginning of the product development or expansion cycle, to think about your intellectual property business strategy.

An individual or members of a team sometimes develop intellectual property within a single organization. Some of the money to be made in intellectual property is in the ability to exploit this information and know-how within your own organization. Think of the Samsung example. Your organization may hold smartphone-related patents, based on your own innovation, which create the freedom of action to develop the smartphone that you have in mind. These patents might also serve as a bargaining chip for a cross-license with a competitor, where you agree to license your rights to them in exchange for a license back to you associated with your rights. Or it might be that you simply have to pay up front for a license, as Apple and RIM presumably did, to build your smartphone. The same might be true if you intend to enter a new market with an existing product, where a competitor has rights in a given country that you seek to enter, since intellectual property rights tend not to be global in nature, unless you invest heavily from the start in obtaining worldwide protections. You would also need to consider, in turn, whether to protect your new innovations as you develop the phone, through both patent and trade secret protection, to stop others in remote jurisdictions from copying your product and flooding the international market with lower-cost imitation goods.

A similar analysis would help you to determine whether you could use a given name to describe your new service. You'll need to choose the brand name carefully, for two reasons. First, you'll be investing a lot in marketing that brand, so you want it to be defensible against others using it in the future. Just as important, you want to avoid someone coming after you for infringing on their right to use a given name in commerce to describe a service—or be prepared to switch to marketing using a new name. You might want to check how your proposed brand name translates into other languages, like the classic example of the Chevy Nova in the Spanish language, which meant "no go." In the digital age, this analysis would extend also to the domain name space, where a search will help determine what domain names you will be able to claim for your product or service. Many organizations will register domain names similar to their own name in order to prevent others from doing so once there's value in the brand—a practice known as "cybersquatting" or "typo-squatting."

This analysis will take you down the road of considering whether to apply for a trademark or service mark, and at what level. It can get expensive to file, maintain, and monitor intellectual property protections in multiple jurisdictions over time—but it can also lead to enormous opportunities in future licensing or other business revenue.

For instance, in a future joint venture or acquisition scenario, the fact that you have perfected your rights in a leading brand might lead to a premium paid by the other side in the deal.

You might consider, instead, whether to license a brand name from someone else in order to help you sell more units or service plans. Perhaps the phone you have in mind is not a full-function smartphone but rather a plastic non-working phone marketed to small children. You will need to stamp a picture of the most popular character for the moment, whether it is Dora the Explorer or Elmo, on the toy to convince kids to pester their parents into buying it. In either of these cases, you'd need a license from the owner of the relevant intellectual property rights to market your plastic phone.

This same intellectual property analysis plays out in a wide range of industries before a product or service can be released for sale or otherwise offered to the public. In the movie business, lawyers and their teams obtain copyright clearance from many different people to put out a feature film; in turn, the movie itself may enable the creators to count on revenues for years to come from licensing aspects of the film. Think of *Star Wars*, for example, and the long tail of revenue that has been generated for the owners of that intellectual property well after the movies have stopped running in the theaters. The same is true for some musical productions and sound recordings, books, and virtually every complex creative endeavor. It's also the case for nonprofit producers of documentary films, like Boston's WGBH, the producer of the award-winning *Frontline* program, among many others.

In each of these instances, the first premise is that you need to acquire the rights to certain intellectual property in order to reap benefits from them later on. In establishing your rights clearly, you create the freedom of action for your organization to enter into new markets with new products. A wide and deep intellectual property portfolio on your balance sheet means you'll have broader freedom of action without new outlays of capital. Whether or not you have to go into the marketplace to buttress the rights that you have, you will need a fairly sophisticated cost-benefit analysis to determine whether and how much to invest on the front end in intellectual property protection or licenses from others. The intellectual property licensing business is big business, with good reason. There's even another layer of the business: insurance and financing issues related to the acquisition and management of intellectual property rights as it becomes clearer that they represent an important asset class.

Just as it is about creating freedom of action to operate and generating revenues, your intellectual property strategy is also about risk reduction. If you are launching a serious new start-up, you wouldn't think of using a do-it-yourself kit from the Internet to form a new corporation if you have big plans. The money spent on lawyers to create a new corporation and divide up the equity is a worthwhile investment against problems down the road. As your company grows, spending money on lawyers to structure equity agreements for new employees and plan for defenses in takeover scenarios is likewise a good investment. The same logic applies when it comes to building an intellectual property portfolio, which can emerge as a key aspect of your overall equity in the business. Each of these investments in lawyers—setting up a company, planning for smooth and continuous operations, and establishing an intellectual property portfolio—functions as a crucial insurance policy for your organization as it grows.

Investments in your intellectual property portfolio reduce risk by establishing greater clarity around what you can do as an organization without violating the rights of others, even in an unintentional way. By amassing intellectual property rights, and registering or publishing information about these assets—whether in ideas, forms of expression, or brands—you establish and retain for your organization the ability to do more or less whatever you like with those rights later. That might mean exploiting them on your own, licensing some or all of those rights to others, or giving the rights freely away to others. Put another way, these investments ensure, first and foremost, that your organization has freedom of action later. As just one example, the documents that you painstakingly get every new employee to

By amassing intellectual property rights, and registering or publishing information about these assets—whether in ideas, forms of expression, or brands—you establish and retain for your organization the ability to do more or less whatever you like with those rights later.

sign—inventor's rights agreements, say—ensure that the work you are paying for redounds to the benefit of your organization, not the start-up that your employee leaves to join. These investments in work related to intellectual property reduce risks that are almost certain to arise in future years while your intellectual property rights are still under the protection of the government-mandated limits on what others can do with them. Even in a nonprofit setting like a university, it can be important to ensure that your employees have signed over some or all of the rights in what they produce to you, unless for some reason you want them to retain those rights.

Up-front investments in intellectual property also can reduce the risk and cost of litigation. In the intellectual property field, litigation is incredibly expensive. Virtually everyone (other than the intellectual property litigators and certain organizations whose business purpose it is to sue others) wishes to avoid intellectual property litigation. The costs of lawsuits are enormously high—let alone the possible costs of negative publicity and the distraction caused by extended litigation. A bill for $3 to $5 million in legal fees per side in a medium-sized matter is common.[6] The possibility of damages—which can reach into the hundreds of millions or even billions of dollars—can easily justify the expenses on the plaintiff's side, and can likewise provide a strong incentive to defendants to negotiate a settlement to avoid a costly courtroom battle. It's not much of a reach to speculate, for example, that Google's large settlement with Yahoo! early in Google's rise to prominence—in which Google transferred about $328 million in stock to Yahoo!—was a function of Google's recognition that the damages could be immense—and Google's own growth stunted—if Yahoo! were to have prevailed.[7]

It should come as no surprise that having certainty in intellectual property rights can lead to earlier and cheaper settlements. Control of intellectual property rights of your own can sometimes even preclude such action in the first place. In cases where both parties know the strength of the other party's rights, the total cost of the transaction—in lawyer's fees and other direct expenses—will likely be lower. The investment that you (and your competitors) make in clearly establishing your intellectual property rights may keep down your lawyer's fees and other costs associated with uncertainty down the road.

Establishing an Intellectual Property Strategy

As a CEO or senior manager of any sort of organization, you should establish a dynamic intellectual property strategy. The strategy needs to be explicit, such that day-to-day decisions can be evaluated against it and so that the decisions drive toward helping you make the right institutional goals. Too much decision making related to intellectual property is made randomly or in a way that is isolated from the whole. This strategy needs to be dynamic so that you are adjusting it over time to take full advantage of the field's fast-changing circumstances, opportunities, and risks. The strategy needs to be nuanced. It has to be tailored to specific types of assets and not a one-size-fits-all formula.

In establishing and implementing such a strategy, consider four core recommendations. First, treat intellectual property as a flexible asset class and manage it accordingly—even when precise valuation is uncertain. Second, be open to ways of using outside intellectual property that was not developed within your organization (in ways that are perfectly legal, of course). Third, consider the primary use of intellectual property as ensuring your own freedom of action to compete effectively, rather than an offensive weapon. And last, establish a mechanism within your organization that guarantees that you remain flexible and develop the capacity for creative foresight with respect to intellectual property strategy over time.

By amassing intellectual property rights, and registering or publishing information about these assets—whether in ideas, forms of expression, or brands—you establish and retain for your organization the ability to do more or less whatever you like with those rights later.

RECOMMENDATION 1

Treat Intellectual Property as a Core Asset Class

Intellectual property is an asset class. You need to treat it that way. When it comes to evaluating the value of your organization's assets, your intellectual property is just as important as other forms of property. If you run a non-profit, you still may keep a balance sheet that classifies your assets and liabilities, which may well include your intellectual property. The valuation of intellectual property could matter a great deal in a wide range of circumstances, such as when you go to get an asset-backed loan, seek insurance, sell your company, or buy someone else's firm from bankruptcy.

This concept of treating intellectual property as an asset class is not new. Big consumer brands—like Coca-Cola—routinely consider "goodwill" or "brand value" as a crucial line item on their balance sheet. The *Wall Street Journal* partners with a company called the Patent Board to report on the relative values of patent portfolios in certain fields. At least once a year, a Chicago-based company called Ocean Tomo holds an auction for patent rights. Banks, venture capitalists, and other investors will sometimes hire outside organizations to evaluate the intellectual property interests of growing companies that they are seeking to invest in or loan money to, which in turn has given rise to a cottage industry in intellectual property valuation.

Part and parcel with the growth of the concept of intellectual property is the notion that we in developed nations operate in an "information" or "knowledge economy." These claims are rarely challenged; we act as though it were a given that we were moving from a world of physical assets to one that is dominated by information, knowledge, and intellectual property. It would seem obvious that a key to success for any organization is what its employees can do, how they relate to the knowledge of their own staff, and how the organization treats the information that drives its business or nonprofit. And yet information and knowledge can be taken for granted when analyzing an organization's value and prospects.

At the same time, it is essential to recognize that intellectual property is different from other kinds of assets on your balance sheet in material ways. Intellectual property can be unstable, making it distinct from your land, building, fleet of trucks, copy machines, or other tangible assets held by your institution. It is, in most respects, a construct of law—law that can change quickly. The field of intellectual property law has been in flux in the United States and around the world in many significant ways over the past few centuries. Even more important, a single ruling by a single judge in a single court potentially could change the value of the assets that you hold in dramatic ways. Consider the effect on Eli Lilly's share price when a federal court declared in 2000 that the patent on the antidepressant drug Prozac was invalid. The value of Eli Lilly's stock plummeted 39 percent immediately after the ruling.

Intellectual property is not exactly "property" in the sense that your real estate or fleet of trucks is property. It is a form of property that can be used by many people at the same time, at virtually no marginal cost. This distinction between intellectual property and other types of property turns out to be critical, and not just in a theoretical sense.

Intellectual property is, at its core, information, which is not exhausted the more that people use it. Consider the information that makes up a computer program. The cost to produce that information is the same whether one person or a million people are running that program. The same is true of an idea (the theory of relativity, for instance), a song, a means of manufacturing something, a way to swing a baseball bat, or a technique for holding the bow that you use to play a cello. Of course, it costs money to produce and distribute the physical objects that one might make based on the idea. There are opportunity costs associated

Intellectual property is, at its core, information, which is not exhausted the more that people use it.

with the process overall. And there are competitive reasons why you may wish to be the only one able to exploit that information. But the use of the information by additional people does not diminish the original idea's utility. The most important difference is that intellectual property is what economists call a "nonrival" good—in other words, more than one party can use it at the same time and get value from it.

In fact, intellectual property often gains in value the more that other people use it. This is an essential conceptual backbone of the argument that I make throughout this book. This insight also points to one of the primary flaws in the full exclusion approach to intellectual property. In some cases, it is clear that having more people using the information that you or your team has created can benefit your organization, even if they don't pay you for the privilege, and even if you are allowed under the law to charge them for it. For instance, Facebook and Twitter are worth billions of dollars more today than they would be if it weren't for so many different kinds of people, companies, and nonprofits integrating their systems with these networks, completely for free, and in ways that Facebook and Twitter could certainly be charging them to do. For a library or museum, the use of digital images from their archives plainly raises the institutions' profile, may drive more people to come through the physical front doors, and may enable their directors to raise more in grant funds for other programs. The value of MIT's assets only increased after it gave away access to the teaching materials from thousands of courses on its OpenCourseWare platform. The more that other people are using this information, which these institutions could more tightly control, the more valuable that information can become.

To understand this distinction between intellectual property and other forms of traditional property, compare the idea of Viacom's Dora the Explorer to the truck that Triumvirate Environmental uses to transport physical materials. Dora's character might be used by multiple companies at once in multiple fields: her image is exploited on a cable program, a Web site, and a lunch box as well as to sell various brands of snacks to children, potentially by multiple organizations, and all simultaneously. A truck, by contrast, can be used only by one organization at a time to carry hazardous waste from the place of manufacture to the place where it is treated. This distinction matters because it may affect how you think about what you can do with your intellectual property. It opens up what can be done with the asset as compared to the traditional forms of assets—like cash and equipment—on your balance sheet.

And at the same time, don't forget that the lasting value from intellectual property assets tends to be created when the intellectual property is applied to a particular innovative service or product. Few organizations have succeeded as pure-play "invention" companies that derive or plan to derive all or most of their revenue from the enforcement of patents. Some people decry organizations that pursue such models as patent trolls. Intellectual property rights do not have to be exclusive; they can be shared in ways that profit multiple parties and benefit consumers. Within a single institution, intellectual property can be exploited in a range of ways. Even a university, at its heart an institution devoted to the development and sharing of knowledge, makes its revenues only in part from the information itself (in the form of royalties and other types of licensing), and more from services and other activities related to it (in the form of tuition, alumni donations, and research grants).

A mixed approach to sharing, licensing, and otherwise charging for the use of your intellectual property—especially patents and copyrights—may lead to the greatest value creation for the organization (not to mention society at large).

Acquiring Intellectual Property

Everyone knows that innovation pays off, whether in business or a nonprofit setting. The Nobel Prize–winning economist Robert Solow has shown that as much as 80 percent of GDP growth is attributable to the introduction of new technologies, for instance.[1] The most innovative companies tend to achieve higher profit-margin growth than the average company. No matter what industry you are in, your organization has to innovate to thrive over long periods.

Innovation on your own is a great way to establish intellectual property rights. But it's not the only way. A joint venture can enable you to work in collaboration with others, even competitors, to move faster than you would on your own and without fear of intellectual property-related risk. It may be possible to pay for a license to use the intellectual property of others that will enable you to enter into a new market. Big companies like Johnson & Johnson, Google, and IBM frequently buy smaller companies to acquire intellectual property as well as the related know-how in a group of engineers or other knowledge workers. And it may be that you can use the intellectual property that others have already developed—without breaking the law.

How to Develop Your Intellectual Property Portfolio

There are many ways to acquire intellectual property. The image of picking up a sword does not help much in thinking about how to build your intellectual property portfolio. A better way is to think about gathering assets into a well-balanced portfolio, which you then manage with care as it grows and changes. The range of options you have for doing so may be broader than you imagine at first blush.

Develop It on Your Own

The simplest, cleanest, most obvious (but not always the most economical) way to acquire intellectual property is to develop it yourself. The brilliant founders of Google— Sergey Brin and Larry Page—developed the origins of the now-famous PageRank algorithm when they were graduate students at Stanford University. From there, they raised capital, hired an extraordinary team, and built one of the world's biggest, most profitable businesses, which continues to grow at a remarkable pace. With the intellectual property of the PageRank algorithm as their ultimate secret sauce and primary fount of fabulous profits, they have amassed a wide-ranging intellectual property portfolio in a range of areas, including computing, publishing, and advertising.

Alas, if you are like the vast majority of us mere mortals, you are probably not quite so bright as either Brin or Page, much less the two of them in combination. It also turns out to be quite hard for large organizations to support the kind of disruptive innovation that tends to come out of tiny teams of brilliant founders, like Google, Facebook, YouTube, Twitter, and so forth.

But perhaps you are a good talent scout and have a knack for building effective teams. You can recognize the up-and-coming leaders in your field—whether in the bio-pharmaceutical industry, Internet, creative arts, libraries, or museums. You recruit well and pay competitively for the services of your high performers. You convince them to sign a watertight agreement granting you all rights in the works that they create while they are working for you. And you structure an environment in which they are motivated to work creatively together toward breakthrough innovations. If you are focused on research and development as a core part of your business, you might build the next iteration of Xerox PARC or Bell Labs. Or you could simply build a team that experiments methodically as it develops your product, establishing product value and creating intellectual property along the way.

Whether on your own or through your staff, the simplest form of intellectual property acquisition is to do it yourself. What is not so simple is how you protect the intellectual property that you've developed—something I'll cover in the next section. Trickier still is what intellectual property you choose to exploit, and how.

Develop It with Others

Human beings are capable of working well in teams. The image of the solo inventor, alone in their garage, cranking out the next big thing, is by and large a myth. Even the biggest thinkers benefit from the stimulation of the thoughts of others. Think not just about inventors but also about the creativity of jazz musicians at a jam session, building new ideas on the fly based on what the other musicians are playing. Even those who work alone at one moment in history do so by standing on the shoulders of those who came before. More often than not, creativity is a collaborative exercise. And there is rarely a reason to believe that your organization, no matter how great at recruitment, has all the answers within your own team.

A second means of acquiring intellectual property is to enter into an agreement with another organization to codevelop a product or service. This technique is more common in some industries than in others, but there is no reason why the practice needs to be limited to any corner of the economy. The joint venture is an underutilized mode of intellectual property protection today in many industries. It shouldn't be.

Imagine a joint venture between your organization and one of your competitors. Perhaps you have developed the leading widget of one sort, and your competitor has developed the leading widget of another—both of which fit into the same larger end product. It may make sense to put your developers in a room together to work on the next generation of a product that will build on your respective leadership in those two areas. Through what are usually called joint development agreements (JDAs)—in essence, joint ventures to develop a specified product or service—you might bring two or more intellectual property portfolios and teams of developers together to innovate in ways that go beyond what you could do within your own organization alone. As one of many possible examples: to position itself for future growth in a competitive industry, Samsung has entered into a JDA with UniPixel to develop a cheaper and high-quality alternative to LCD and LED technology that can be incorporated into smartphone technology.[2]

The agreement that you enter into with your competitor would accomplish a range of things enabling you to develop the new intellectual property together. You would specify what each of you would contribute to the joint venture in terms of staff time and funding. You would work out how to split the profits from your collaboration. And you would almost certainly agree not to sue one another for any intellectual property infringement that might occur in the context of your collaboration—what lawyers call a "covenant not to sue." If done right, the net effect of such an agreement for both organizations will be increased profits and market share as well as enhancements to your respective intellectual property portfolios.

JDAs come in many forms. For instance, Sirius and XM Radio entered into a JDA for the purpose of developing a unified standard for satellite radios with the goal of "accelerat[ing] growth of the satellite radio category by enabling consumers to purchase one radio capable of receiving both companies' broadcasts."[3] Under this agreement, each company would have joint ownership of any jointly developed interoperability technology.[4] It's not always the case that fierce competitors agree to work together. Antitrust law can limit this kind of agreement if the combination of the two organizations threatens to create an anticompetitive situation. But it can enable competitors to work to build an industry together—to grow the pie rather than fighting over how it is sliced up—with intellectual property as the common ground.

Sometimes organizations that collaborate by developing intellectual property together come from different market positions. Take the agreement between British Petroleum (BP) and Martek Biosciences Corporation to work on the production of microbial oils for biofuels applications. BP agreed to foot much of the bill, ten million dollars, for the collaboration. In return, BP would own all intellectual property developed during the JDA. Martek received an exclusive license for use of jointly developed technologies for application and commercialization in nutrition, cosmetic, and pharmaceutical uses. Moreover, under their JDA, each party is entitled to certain payments from technology commercialized in the other party's field.[5]

These types of agreements help organizations, whether they are competitors or complements, to grow their intellectual property portfolios in ways that would not be possible using only their own staff. And by leveraging the strength of partner organizations, companies like BP can get to market more quickly with important new products and services.

License It from Others

A third way to garner intellectual property is to license it from someone else. Let's imagine that you are in the business of manufacturing lunch boxes for schoolchildren. You are not in the design or creativity business. You know how to pound metal into the right shape. You know how to get that metal into the stream of commerce and, logistically at least, every public school cafeteria in the United States. In fact, you are terrific at doing just that. You could make a plain, metal lunch box and get it into the hands of a school-age child more cheaply than anyone else in the economy.

But you have no idea what might appeal to your seven-year-old customer, or their parents and grandparents. You know that without help, your product would sit on shelves gathering dust while your competitor's lunch boxes were getting filled with peanut butter and jelly sandwiches, cookies, and juice boxes.

To solve your problem, you call up a broker for a consumer goods company that licenses the rights to print the images of characters that children like on to your lunch boxes. If you are aiming for the big time, you might consider Elmo and Big Bird from *Sesame Street*, Dora the Explorer from Nick Jr., or Mickey Mouse and friends from Disney. All of a sudden, you have a hit product, leaping off the shelves of Target and Walmart. (Or perhaps it happens to you the other way around: depending on the economy, you might get a call from a broker for one of these companies, wondering if you want to lend your own expertise to bringing a product to market that carries their brand.)

Many of the world's mightiest organizations license intellectual property from others. Procter & Gamble, the makers of the children's diapers Pampers, licenses the use of *Sesame Street* characters, Dora the Explorer, and Bob the Builder, for instance. The competing diapers, from Huggies, feature Disney characters, among others. Lower-cost brands of diapers, such as the store brands for chain drugstores like CVS and Rite Aid, tend to have lesser-known or no characters at all on them. In each of these instances, the makers of the diapers consider whether they will be able to sell more products by taking a license from a well-known brand. For the company licensing the brand, the deal is likely all upside.

You might look in places that others don't in order to license intellectual property. Most major research universities today have a technology-transfer office established to license innovations developed on campus to those in the private sector that would exploit them. This process works. Stanford has reaped billions of dollars from technology developed in its computer science laboratories, for example, because the intellectual property helps lead to massive profits and big new companies. MIT, Carnegie

Mellon University, Rice University, and many other technology-focused universities have developed similar programs with great success.

The government can be another good—though often overlooked—source of intellectual property to license. Each year, the US government pays as much as twenty billion dollars for research by federal employees, and more than sixty billion dollars for research through grants and contracts to outside parties. Though they are not yet as sophisticated as Stanford and MIT in the technology-transfer business, the US government has made concerted efforts to license technologies that it has paid those of us in the private sector to develop.[6]

Publicly funded basic and clinical research are complementary to pharmaceutical research and development, and have been shown to stimulate private industry investment in the pharmaceutical sector.[7] For example, the National Institute of Standards and Technology recently licensed novel technologies to ELIA Life Technology Inc. in an effort to bring affordable graphic reading systems for the blind and visually impaired to market.[8] This is a little-known and little-used strategy, and it's doubtful that it will help you if you sell lunch boxes or diapers. But your organization might well benefit from the expenditure of public funds for research if your business is in fields that relate to technology or defense.[9]

As a final note about licensing intellectual property into your organization, you might need to determine whether there is a patent aggregator operating in your critical path. The largest example of such a firm is Intellectual Ventures, established by former Microsoft executive Nathan Myrhvolds. This firm has aggregated more than thirty thousand patents in a wide variety of fields and has generated over two billion dollars in licensing revenues. In late 2010, Intellectual Ventures filed its first three lawsuits against firms that appear not to have signed licenses with Intellectual Ventures.[10] Other, smaller-scale firms have emerged that are pursuing similar models. It may be important to make a determination as to whether to work with such firms or work around their patent holdings.

Buy It, by Acquiring a Company or Part of Its Assets
A fourth way to acquire intellectual property is to merge with or buy an organization that has amassed a terrific portfolio. This process happens all the time in the pharmaceutical industry. One of the primary exits for investors in small pharmaceutical organizations is to sell the company to a much-larger competitor that seeks to add its intellectual property to their portfolio and their prospective drugs to their pipeline. The same is true in the information and communications technology sector. For instance, IBM paid $1.1 billion to acquire Ascential Software Corporation in

2005, with a view toward incorporating its rich intellectual property portfolio, in addition to its software, into its own portfolio.

It's not necessary to purchase the entire company in order to acquire the intellectual property assets outright. The right deal might be something in between a full acquisition of an organization and a simple nonexclusive license to a particular aspect of its intellectual property portfolio. Increasingly, organizations are considering asset sales of part or all of an intellectual property portfolio rather than full acquisitions of other companies.

These assets also might include intellectual property in forms that someone might not initially expect. Asset sales of intellectual property routinely involve value paid for trademarks, copyrights, and patents of all sorts, but also of customer lists and general employee know-how, which can be obtained by hiring staff from the target organization. The best-organized buyer will get the most value out of an asset deal by thinking strategically about what they seek from the transaction. On the other side of the equation, the seller can obtain the best value by being organized about what they hold in terms of intellectual property, how they organize it, and how to make the most of its value in the context of a transaction with a buyer or lender as part of an asset-backed loan.

Consider the case of Luna Innovations Inc., which was preparing to emerge from bankruptcy. As part of its strategy to reinsert itself into the nanomedicine market, Luna entered into a deal to acquire the intellectual property portfolio of Tego Biosciences Inc., a rival competitor. This agreement involved an up-front lump-sum payment and payments totaling $4.25 million for reaching certain milestones in bringing various products to market using the Tego assets. Luna's chief operating officer noted that this deal "just strengthens our position in this whole space of nanomedicine . . . [and] just locks in the intellectual property for us so we can sit down with the big pharmaceutical companies."[11]

Protecting Your Intellectual Property

Once you have acquired the basis for your intellectual property portfolio, there is still the hard work ahead of managing, protecting, and growing it. As the early experiences of Xerox PARC show, there is much more to long-term success in an innovative field than simply assembling cutting-edge innovators. You have to know that you have established valuable assets (in PARC's case, in the form of ideas for the personal computer or personal printer) and understand how to exploit those assets.[12]

The management of an intellectual property portfolio may seem like an obvious step, but too many organizations skip it. The idea of managing an intellectual property portfolio may seem as dry as toast; perhaps it is. But there is more to managing your intellectual property than simply owning it and keeping up with your filing fees. The organizations with the most effective intellectual property strategies put a capable person or team of people in charge of understanding precisely what the organization has, ensuring that it is protected, and managing how the rights are enforced or otherwise exploited. The process of cataloging and then keeping track of your organization's intellectual property is an essential starting point.

From there, you have a series of hard decisions to make. How much time and money do you want to spend to protect the intellectual property that you have? In a few respects, your intellectual property may be protected automatically. In the case of expressive works—such as a screenplay you write, a map that you publish, or even a Web site that you launch—your organization's creations are copyrighted automatically in the United States, so long as they meet a few basic criteria. But in all likelihood, you still will want to spend the money to register these works with the copyright office. For one thing, doing so puts other people on notice that you hold these rights. You also will likely be able to get more in the way of damages in the event that someone infringes your rights in the works that you've created.

When it comes to your brand and other marks that you develop, the analysis is a bit more complex. For trademarks, you get certain defensive rights merely by intending to use and then using your works in a commercial setting under US law. Yet it will pay off to register them—by field of use as well as state or country. The business of registering trademarks internationally is important if you intend to start a licensing business based on these rights. If you aspire to be the next Coca-Cola, Disney, or Google, you need to get this process right from the beginning.

In the case of patents, the stakes and costs of protecting your intellectual property are higher. The matter of what to protect is deeply complicated. The process of patenting your ideas or business methods is long and expensive. In the United States, the process can take several years or more depending on competing claims.[13] The costs range from the tens of thousands to the millions of dollars to establish your rights, depending on the size and complexity of your filing. And then there's the international dimension to take into account. Much turns on how good your lawyers and strategists are. For the purposes of this book: if you wish to be a major player in the patent business, hire carefully and be prepared to pay up.

Central Admixture Pharmacy Services Inc. learned this lesson the hard way. A misspelled word in its patent ("osmolarity" instead of "osmolality") led to the dismissal of its otherwise-valid claims against an infringing company.[14] Smaller companies are not the only ones that get into trouble here. Xerox PARC provides an instructive example. Long after it had developed and failed to commercialize desktop computer technology (known as GUI), Xerox realized that the Apple Macintosh and its progeny might be violating Xerox's rights by appropriating the look and feel of the Xerox GUI. Xerox filed suit, but the lawsuit was dismissed because Xerox had waited too long to file and the statute of limitations had expired.

It is worth noting, too, that even if you wish to give away or otherwise license your intellectual property—sometimes a good business decision, as we'll see in the next section—you first need to establish rights in it to do so. You can't give away something in which you don't have ownership rights. So even if you disfavor the full exclusion mode of intellectual property exploitation, you need to establish your intellectual property portfolio beforehand. It may seem counterintuitive, but even the strategies of openness that I urge you to consider need to be grounded first in the system of rights in order to work smoothly.

The core point of this recommendation is to develop a strategy along with a team devoted to pulling together your intellectual property into an asset base that you can use to your maximum advantage. This is true no matter what line of business you're in, and whether you're a nonprofit or for-profit. Once you understand your intellectual property assets, you have a much better chance of using them to the fullest advantage—whatever that may prove to be over time. While no company wants to prepare for failure, an entity that has cataloged, protected, and valued its intellectual property assets will have an easier time negotiating with creditors. For entities that are growing and thriving, there are myriad ways in which intellectual property can help you accomplish your goals. If you have your house in order, you are more likely to be able to put intellectual property to optimal use for your organization.

RECOMMENDATION 2

Benefit from the Intellectual Property of Others—Legally

The second recommendation is: be open and alert to what your customers, competitors, and others can offer you in terms of intellectual property. One of the big changes in intellectual property is the fast growth of possibilities for building your business in part on the intellectual property of others. The primary way to do so is to license it directly. But there are other ways too. The most promising approach comes from the field of open innovation.

Sometimes there are limits to what you can license from others. For instance, the intellectual property's holder might simply refuse your offer to partner with them or grant you a license. Most of the time, that's their right. There also might be limitations on how extensively big organizations can license their intellectual property rights to one another under antitrust laws. This area of law—at the intersection of intellectual property and law as well as policy relating to competition—is highly complex, changing quickly, and hotly contested. For my purposes here, suffice it to say that there might be a limit to what you can do with licensing if the effect could be viewed as anticompetitive.

You can always try to license someone else's intellectual property to use it in your own business. But what can you do with the intellectual property of others when you don't have—or can't get—a license? The answer sometimes is "nothing." In other cases, however, you might consider some interesting approaches, which may prove helpful to your business.

The strategic questions to ask are: Where is innovation happening, and how can my organization make the most of it—whether or not my own employees come up with the insight? Might it make good business sense to share nicely?

The most profitable form of building on the intellectual property of others may prove to be participation in a development process called open innovation. Customers are increasingly showing that they're willing to give you intellectual property that you can use to your benefit. Customers are open to participating in the design process for products that they love, whether a mountain bike, Web browser, camera, or shirt. The term "beta testing," initially popularized in the IT sector, is now commonly used across business and nonprofit sectors as a key part of the innovation process, involving customers and benefiting from their knowledge. Your customers are self-interested, just as your organization is: customers who help to improve a product through their feedback not only feel good about helping out but also get the benefits of that improvement in their everyday lives once they have paid you for it.

Companies in highly diverse fields have exploited the ideas, knowledge base, and enthusiasm of their customers. These companies range from IBM (conducting online "Innovation Jams" where clients, consultants, and employees' family members tinker with its technologies in pursuit of new ideas), to LEGO (whereby LEGO has "outsourced" innovation responsibilities for its Mindstorms projects to a panel of knowledgeable customers and "citizen developers"), to PETCO (partnering with Bazaarvoice to implement customer ratings and reviews on PETCO.com along with an automated feed of negative and customer-service reviews to the customer-service team in order to identify and respond to their influencers; as the review volume rose, PETCO.com noticed that reviews were lowering returns for several products).[1]

Build on What Others Are Doing When They Offer It Up Broadly

Google's search system is built on thousands of machines running the open-source operating system called Linux.

Whenever we use the World Wide Web, we rely on intellectual property that Tim Berners-Lee came up with—and then didn't seek payment for our usage. Examples of building on the work of others, especially in the IT space, are legion. You don't always have to own all your own code to create extraordinary businesses. And the benefits of building on someone else's code can benefit all parties involved.

The biggest opportunity for this type of development is on the Internet. A key element of the recent explosion in Web development known as Web 2.0 is a phenomenon whereby companies open up their systems to make them interoperable with systems that others develop. Much of the time, organizations will not offer a negotiable license but instead will present opportunities for anyone to come along and take advantage of aspects of their intellectual property. These companies—ranging from Google to Amazon to Facebook—freely offer the opportunity to develop systems that build on and can be integrated with their intellectual property.

Intellectual property law protects many of Google's services. At the same time, Google lets all comers use aspects of that intellectual property to build further. The theoretical concept, introduced by Harvard Law professor Jonathan Zittrain, is called generativity. The idea is that one company offers a certain layer of the Internet to others to keep building on top of or alongside it. Generative tools are ones that enable others to generate the next set of innovations.

Take Zillow, for instance. It is an online real estate database that appraises property values using publicly available data (e.g., property tax valuation, historic sales data, recent sales, market comparison information, and per-square-foot cost data). Zillow also uses Microsoft's Virtual Earth mapping technology and bird's-eye view photography to allow potential home buyers to more clearly see architectural design, landscaping, neighboring properties, and other factors. Essentially, Zillow is a "mashup" site: by employing freely available Web technology and publicly available information to create a powerful and functional user interface, Zillow has created an innovative proprietary system of its own. You don't always have to create all or even most of the IP to make a profitable venture (in the Web services space, anyway).

The most explosive growth story in the Internet and mobile communications business today is driven by customers and third parties collaborating to develop a platform controlled by big software companies, like Facebook and Apple. Apple has cleverly tapped into the creativity and enthusiasm of iPhone users and software developers at large, creating the iPhone Development Center to spur the development of iPhone, iPod, and iPad applications. The applications are in turn sold through the Apple iTunes Store.[2] Hundreds of millions of applications have been sold, generating significant revenues for both Apple and independent developers—and helping to sell yet more hardware, as customers seek the best devices to access the applications. Google's platform for developing applications for its Android phones is even more open than Apple's environment for iPhone development. Livescribe, the makers of the Pulse Smartpen, has taken a similar approach to increase the functionality and marketability of its product.[3]

This is the phenomenon of the Open Application Programming Interfaces, or Open API. The idea is that multiple players participate in a broadly open ecosystem of developing, using, and refining computer applications as well as the data that flow between them. These APIs enable organizations to offer access to their platforms without taking enormous risks or offering much in the way of support. From the perspective of those who develop on these platforms, APIs can provide important shortcuts that help avoid reinventing the wheel on the way toward offering customers breakthrough products. There are good reasons why Facebook wants people to develop highly creative applications that can reside on its system, why Apple and Google encourage smartphone applications, and why Microsoft wants people to develop applications that run on Windows or use its .net development platform. The network effects that can emerge are enormously valuable to Facebook, Apple, Google, and Microsoft. Those who have been slower to enable others to build on their platforms—such as RIM, in the smartphone market—are scrambling quickly to catch up with the leaders.

For all the excitement of this mode of development and growth, there are risks involved. When one organization offers access to its systems to others, that organization may experience unforeseen outcomes. From the perspective of the organization that relies on the Open API, it runs the risk that the organization offering the service (say, Facebook, Apple, or Microsoft) might unexpectedly pull the rug out from under them.[4] The promise of this emerging ecosystem is tremendous, but the full implications of this mode of interreliance remain to be seen.

Encouraging Other People, including Your Customers, to Do It for You

The "social Web" environment online is the best example of these kinds of emerging ecosystems. A large number of organizations—big and small—are codeveloping a world that consumers are flocking toward in large numbers. The phenomena of YouTube, Facebook, Twitter, and Google are all building off one another. Each of these organizations offers opportunities to integrate your intellectual property with their intellectual property in ways that stand to benefit both organizations.

This dynamic—the "combining [of] internal and external ideas as well as internal and external paths to market to advance the development of new technologies"—is core to the idea of open innovation.[5] It is occurring in a subset of fields, but has application for many more areas than those that are currently exploiting it. Recent advances in IT have made the frictionless sharing of experiences and lawyer-free integration of platforms possible. As with anything new and promising, there are risks involved. But the rewards are also terrific.

The idea behind open innovation is as simple as it is powerful: the creators of new ideas don't have to be within your organization in order to be helpful. Traditionally, businesses have been loath to listen to the ideas of people who didn't work at the organization—a reluctance that was partially grounded in a fear of future demands for compensation on the part of customers proffering those ideas. A growing number of businesses today are open to ideas that customers and others freely send their way. The possibility of a breakthrough product or tweak to a service that helps you maintain the distance between you and your competitor is growing.

Consider Procter & Gamble. In years past, it kept its product development processes highly secretive and rarely interacted with outsiders until a product hit the shelves. Today, its external affairs manager is encouraging inventors to call up with new product ideas.[6] GE Plastics has

The idea behind open innovation is as simple as it is powerful: the creators of new ideas don't have to be within your organization in order to be helpful.

taken a similar route, regaining profitability and global market share by encouraging customers to create as well as share their own custom colors and finishes.[7]

On the Web, this process is even more common. When Microsoft was about to roll out a new version of its Web browser, Internet Explorer 7, the product team released it in a public "open beta" process to its customers. Microsoft got valuable feedback from a wide range of customers, which it then incorporated into the final version of what turned out to be a strong product. A similar process took place with Google Wave, a product that allowed users to have online conversations and work on shared documents in real time. Google asked users to preview Google Wave, suggest improvements, and vote on the suggestions of other users. Zillow—whose autogenerated "Zestimate" only approximates what the market will bear for a given property—encourages its users to update facts about their homes or neighborhoods in order to increase its accuracy and usefulness.

Eli Lilly recognized that the Internet presented the opportunity to tap into the innovative potential of individuals and groups all over the world. It started InnoCentive (now an independent organization) to draw on the wisdom of the crowds. InnoCentive allows a company to post problems to which it would like a solution (known as "challenges") to its Web site. "Solvers," who number almost 180,000, compete to win cash "prizes" offered by the company posting the challenge. In this way, a company taps into a broad "inventor pool for which it can pay for value in generative innovative work while acquiring the IP rights as part of the purchase."[8] Roughly 900 challenges have been posted so far by some 150 organizations, including big multinationals such as Procter & Gamble and Dow Chemicals. Nearly half—about 400—have been solved.[9]

Pets have been the beneficiaries of open innovation, too. To determine how it should make, package, and sell dog food, Del Monte Foods created a private online community called "I love my dogs/Dogs are people too." Through this forum Del Monte heard the desires and concerns of dedicated pet owners, offered them examples of potential products and product packaging, and incorporated these suggestions and criticisms into a successful line of dog "breakfast" food.

In the fashion world, Spreadshirt has created a global apparel company by letting its customers design the clothes they buy. Spreadshirt provides its customers with a well-designed Web infrastructure and custom-manufacturing expertise, and from there its customers (which include other Web sites, CNN, other clothing companies, and individual consumers) can determine just what clothing Spreadshirt will produce, and on what scale. Spreadshirt's business model makes sense: if you let customers decide what they want for the same cost as having them choose what's available (off a rack), they're certain to choose their own design, or at least one they feel they can claim. Spreadshirt's innovative team also actively seeks to reinforce its customers' feelings of ownership over the company's products and development. For example, Spreadshirt "crowdsourced" its logo (created a contest whereby it would select its logo from designs submitted by users) and sponsored monthly design contests. Spreadshirt profits directly from the creativity of its users while building deep connections to the community that is excited about its products.

Why are customers willing to help? Self-interest is a core motivation, of course. Many people enjoy creating things, and feel empowered when they are rewarded for doing so. That's one of the core lessons of the explosion of Web 2.0 services and the user-generated content movement online. But people also want better products. Many people think they know better than you do. So let them try. And maybe they are right. You still have to sift through their ideas, and then figure out which ones to listen to and which ones to incorporate. You remain the boss. But an open innovation strategy can lead to important refinements to products and services as well as ideas for entirely new offerings.

Such a strategy can also help your brand image. Microsoft, for example, ran advertisements for Windows 7 that emphasize the operating system as customer driven and customer responsive (the commercials end with a customer saying, "I'm a PC, and Windows 7 was my idea"). The appeal to connect to its customers in these advertisements is obvious. The strategy seems to have worked, as adoption of Windows 7 and the public reaction it received far outstripped the troubled Vista release that preceded it.

The Fair Use Economy and Material from the Public Domain

Sometimes the law permits you to use aspects of the intellectual property of others without an explicit license. Most intellectual property regimes have what are called "exceptions and limitations," especially with respect to copyright law. Under US law, for instance, there are certain fair uses of copyrighted materials. This section of the law is complicated and fact specific. In order to know if you can make fair use of someone else's copyrighted materials, you have to consider a four-factor balancing test. Copyright experts joke that fair use is "the right to hire a lawyer."

To build a business on the intellectual property of others is to be a high-wire artist. The service MP3.com managed the act for a short while and then fell hard to the ground, as did various peer-to-peer file-sharing services that facilitated broad access to copyrighted music files. Google and its subsidiary YouTube, by contrast, continue to soar. Google has its own core set of intellectual property, to be sure, from which it sets itself apart from competing search companies. But it also has no business without the existence of all the copyrighted material on the Web around the world. YouTube, too, does not develop its own copyrighted video content. It provides a service for others to post video and associated audio content online. In crucial respects, both of these companies rely on the explicit or implicit right to supply a service on top of the aggregated intellectual property of many others. That's not to say they haven't been challenged: both Google and YouTube have been sued by a raft of major and minor companies for copyright violations—and so far, they've been successful at making the case that their core practices are legal.

There are other limitations to intellectual property rights that may be relevant to your business interests. For instance, rights in intellectual property tend to run out over time. This is true with respect to patents, which often have particularly short terms. Copyrighted materials fall into the public domain after a somewhat longer period as well. Trademark-related rights fail from a lack of continued use in business.

Some business models build on this intellectual property that has become the property of the public. Generic drug organizations contend that they saved US consumers $734 billion over the past decade alone.[10] Leading members of Congress, such as Representative Henry Waxman, have called for extending rights to organizations that make biogenerics and curbing the rights of the pharmaceutical giants.[11] Again setting aside the politics, there is a vibrant industry that produces goods and services for consumers based on the intellectual property of others. Law reform in patent might improve the prospects of such organizations over time.

This phenomenon may be especially true for companies looking to expand internationally. Sustained critiques of the impact of patents on access to lifesaving drugs in developing countries are likely to affect international and domestic laws as well as norms regarding patents in the medium to long term. Developing countries increasingly employ domestic compulsory licensing laws (and this use has been explicitly suggested and condoned by the World Trade Organization, among other international bodies), and countries like Canada and India engage in significant international trade in generic pharmaceuticals. Commentators have called for more radical changes, such as instituting a prize system here in the United States whereby the government pays pharmaceutical companies a prize for their developments instead of granting them patent rights, or using "Equitable Access" licenses whereby patented information is available for free use in certain contexts.[12] As the ability of pharmaceutical giants to enforce their intellectual property in foreign markets wanes, generic producers will likely see increased opportunities to use the propriety information of others.

Even large, established biotechnology companies are getting into the act of sharing intellectual property. In a sharp break from past practices, Novartis and Merck have both established units to develop generic versions of drugs. The notion, for Merck, is to develop "follow-on biologics" that compete with its competitors' best-selling drugs. Merck's plans include a first product, an antianemia drug, set to launch in 2012, with at least five other generics on the market by 2017.[13]

In the content business, this strategy is even easier to observe. Lexis and Westlaw make billions of dollars per year selling access to high-end databases to lawyers and others interested in understanding the law. A key part of what they sell is an excellent package of tools and enhancements that help researchers and lawyers find as well as interpret the US government's laws—all of which are, by statute, in the public domain. Dover Publications sells print media that is otherwise in the public domain. Disney has made millions, if not billions, of dollars by repackaging traditional stories in the public domain into modern classics. Disney does far more than Dover by adding its magic to the story rather than simply reprinting the original text. But in both cases, the premise of working from public domain material is the same.

Another way to think about fair use and the importance of public domain materials, taken together, is the overall benefits that the reliance on this doctrine provides to the economy at large. The fair use economy is comprised of the series of economic actors who rely on the use of the copyrighted materials of others to provide goods and services to their customers. The best examples are Internet companies, such as search engines, that enable their customers to find information that others have created and render advertisements that are relevant to those who are searching for that information. Other instances of institutions that rely on fair use include device manufacturers that enable people to make lawful copies of the copyrighted works of others. According to a recent study commissioned by industry groups, the fair use economy in the United States supports hundreds of billions of dollars in exports, employs millions of people, and is growing by 5 percent a year or more.[14] These fair use economy companies, the study's authors contend, have grown at a rate that far exceeds that of companies in other industries in recent years.

The strategy of using intellectual property in the public domain or based on fair use is not relevant for every business. Yet it emphasizes an important, larger point: the extent to which organizations might benefit from looking beyond the knowledge amassed by their own employees in seeking to get a profitable service or product to market.

RECOMMENDATION 3

Create Freedom of Action through Intellectual Property

The third recommendation is: start with the premise that intellectual property is most valuable insofar as it creates freedom of action for your organization rather than as an offensive weapon against others. In doing so, recognize also the extent to which your brand may be wrapped up in your intellectual property. This is another strong reason why the battlefield metaphor can distract you if you rely on it to the exclusion of other conceptions of intellectual property. And this part of the argument applies equally to any kind of organization, whether a for- or nonprofit one.

There are many kinds of freedom of action that intellectual property can help establish for your organization. I'll highlight three here.

The first is the most obvious and important: if you hold intellectual property, you can choose whether to exploit it in the marketplace or do something else with it. If you don't gain these rights initially, you may be frustrated in terms of what markets you want to enter, what deals you want to do, or how you want to relate to your customers or competitors, patrons or students, listeners or visitors. The asset class of intellectual property is fundamentally about ensuring that you can compete when and how you think best for your organization.

The Samsung smartphone example is instructive here. The most significant aspect of intellectual property assets is their ability to enable your organization to compete in the manner and at the time you wish to do so. Before Samsung—or any other device maker for that matter—could take on Apple and RIM in the smartphone market, Samsung's executives had to analyze its intellectual property assets, determine whether there was a shortfall in terms of the rights they had amassed to date, make decisions about whether to aggregate more assets, and then integrate the process of design into the process of assessing the risk of entering the market with an incomplete set of rights. This is one of the primary jobs of the intellectual property strategist: to work closely with engineers and their managers to determine if what they want to do will result in a trip to the courthouse to fight with a competitor over whether they've got the right to enter the marketplace with their new product or service. The difference in the experience of an organization that is able to enter a new market successfully and one that is held up by a lawsuit, demanding an injunction against the introduction of a product or service, is vast.

In some industries, huge patent portfolios have created a détente between large organizations, where one cannot sue another for patent infringement because too many of their own products violate the intellectual property rights of the organization that they were considering suing. The intellectual property regime is sustainable and effective where it creates the ability for you, and your partners and licensees, to do something.

A second form of freedom of action enabled by intellectual property is tightly related to knowledge management. Intellectual property can help your organization to function more effectively. For the intellectual property you have developed within your organization, its primary function may be simply to help your organization to do its work better. Intellectual property, for instance, can help you to become an increasingly data-driven enterprise. The data that your organization collects about its own work along with the actions of your customers or competitors may not be something that you sell as analytics but it also may be the crucial grist for the mill of cost cutting, development of new markets and products, or simple process improvements along the way. Put differently, the process of knowledge management—a field unto itself—is central to a great organization's productivity, even if it does not seem to affect anything external to the company such as revenues in a direct way. Your organization's intellectual property strategy should be integrated with your knowledge management strategy in ways that support the organization's operations and growth.

Last, your intellectual property is inextricably linked to how you establish, manage, and use your brand as an organization. The person responsible for your intellectual property strategy ought to have a strong connection to the person responsible for your brand image. These concepts are related in ways that matter a great deal to the value assigned to your organization and your relationships with your customers. The obvious connection between intellectual property and brand is through the trademarks you own.

It's important to appreciate from the start the extent to which your brand value is intertwined with intellectual property rights. The way that you treat your intellectual property can affect how your customers and others in the marketplace come to view your organization. For a large, admired organization—think of Johnson & Johnson, General Electric, the New York Public Library, the Guggenheim Museum, and the Louvre—its brand itself is among its greatest assets. The organization's brand is integral to its overall enterprise value. The trademark of an iconic organization like Johnson & Johnson is enormously valuable, as are individual product trademarks, such as Band-Aid (evoking safety and reliability in treating minor wounds, for instance) or Neutrogena (evoking cleanliness and a certain stylishness). These trademarks have value because they convey trust, and stand for a positive relationship between customers and products developed over many years.

The clever use of your intellectual property can also help to burnish your brand, company's reputation, and relationship to your customers without fear of misappropriation or interference with your brand's long-term value to your organization. On Twitter, the broad platform that allows users to post messages of 140 characters or less, people play an open, unstructured game called "What Disney show are you?" Users of Twitter use a code known as a hashtag to associate their username with the name of particular Disney shows. This game offers Disney executives terrific insight into their customer base, draws connections between their intellectual property and their customers, and builds brand awareness across properties. Such a strategy draws on the concept of crowdsourcing not just as an intellectual property-gathering strategy but also as a manner of building relationships with a community in service of brand development.

But in other respects, this recommendation is extremely tricky. The hard part is to determine when and how to enforce your intellectual property if someone else appears to be violating your rights. There is a tension here that cannot be wished away, between protecting what's rightly yours to control and letting others make use of your assets.

There are many reasons why an organization may choose to enforce its intellectual property rights to the fullest extent that the law allows when third parties violate those rights. From a public relations standpoint, though, it's equally important to know when not to overreach. Sometimes, the best way to improve your brand is to give away or license intellectual property to others, or look the other way when your intellectual property is violated.[1] Your lawyer will be able to give you a better sense of the risks if you decline to enforce your rights in a given instance; it is important to ask. There's no reason why having a strong intellectual property strategy means you have to become an enterprise known as a bully. Sharing can be good for a brand. It is also good to be known as a fair player in the marketplace—honestly licensing to and from others for the benefit not just of the organizations involved but your customers too.

Consider the cautionary tale of Disney and the piñatas in South Central Los Angeles.[2] Disney and four other organizations filed copyright and trademark lawsuits against small businesses that sold Winnie the Pooh piñatas for childrens' birthdays from stores with dirt floors. The story of these lawsuits traveled far and wide due to coverage in the *Los Angeles Times*. Similarly, a Web site called UnhappyBirthday.com advocates against Time Warner for "actively" enforcing its copyright interest in the song "Happy Birthday."[3] In the mid-1990s, the American Society

Sharing can be good for a brand. It is also good to be known as a fair player in the marketplace —honestly licensing to and from others for the benefit not just of the organizations involved but your customers too.

of Composers, Authors, and Publishers ran into a public relations quagmire concerning whether it threatened Girl Scout leaders with lawsuits over campfire singing.[4]

And sometimes the licensing of your brand can include risks. If you let someone else use your brand, they may do something with it that brings trouble to you and your company. Consider the experience of Yahoo! in licensing its brand to a Chinese partner, Alibaba. When the Chinese police used data from a Yahoo! mail account held by muckraking journalist Shi Tao as part of the evidence to jail him, Yahoo! suffered from a public relations, government relations, and legal nightmare. Yahoo! executives in Sunnyvale, California, claim they had little to do with the incident, but the costs of the damage were paid mostly by the company at large, not its partner operating the local brand in China.[5] In licensing your brand to others, you may be limiting your ability to build long-term value in the brand directly as well—in other words, you potentially may be limiting your freedom of action in the future, depending on how you structure the deal.

You may also run a degree of risk if you overreach in trying to protect intellectual property that is not yours, or not yours alone. Starbucks ran into a problem when the coffee company sought to establish a trademark in some of the most famous coffee brand names in Ethiopia. The company included the word "Sidamo" in one of its trademark applications in the United States. Starbucks was also accused of working through a trade association to oppose Ethiopian coffee growers' ability to establish formal trademark interests in these names in the United States. Whatever role the company in fact played in the process, the news media reported widely that Starbucks was costing Ethiopian coffee farmers hundreds of millions of dollars per year through bullying tactics related to intellectual property.[6] The perception of overreach was sharply at odds with Starbucks' efforts to promote itself as a socially conscious company on a global scale.

The core concept is that intellectual property assets should be developed, managed, and used in a way that emphasizes ongoing freedom of action for your organization. In other words, don't let intellectual property get in the way of achieving your core goals. It can become a distraction for some organizations instead of a driver to get you where you want to go. You may make a short-term, revenue-oriented decision to maximize your return on these assets, but you should do so with your eyes open about the longer-term consequences of those actions. The freedom that you can gain or give up in the longer run is often the most important thing to bear in mind when you are making day-to-day decisions about your intellectual property.

RECOMMENDATION 4

Establish a Flexible Intellectual Property Strategy

Now you've got a handle on your growing intellectual property portfolio. You've gotten each of your key, creative employees to sign well-crafted employment agreements. Your portfolio includes a slew of patents, many copyrighted works, many trade secrets, and a few crucial trademarks and service marks—and there's more in the pipeline.

The hardest question of all is what to do with the intellectual property in your portfolio. Here's where the metaphor of the sword and the shield completely breaks down. Yes, you can use it to protect yourself from others or harm your competitors. But there's much more to be done with your intellectual property than that.

You have a broad range of choices in terms of what to do with your intellectual property. One size does not fit all. Your approach might range from fully excluding others to freely allowing use of your intellectual property by others. Some of the most successful businesses adopt different approaches to different aspects of their intellectual property, depending on the circumstances. For many organizations, this blended approach is the optimal way to compete.

Your strategic starting point should instead be a model of limited exclusion: Is there a way to license your intellectual property to others in a manner that will help your business thrive over time? While this premise works best in certain contexts (say, for a patent in the computing industry), it applies in varying degrees to copyright and trademark interests as well.

The opportunities afforded by the licensing market in intellectual property—whether you are a buyer or seller—are worth considering across your intellectual property portfolio. And nontraditional modes of acquiring and sharing intellectual property may serve your business in surprising ways. The most innovative organizations in any given market often have the most innovative intellectual property strategies.

For the intellectual property rights that you have acquired by license, the answer tends to be simple. Just use the rights for which you have paid. You've licensed the rights to Dora the Explorer on your product for kids, and you do exactly as the license says—no more, no less. That's the easiest answer. The corollary to using intellectual property rights that you develop is to simply use them yourself and don't worry much about what anyone else is doing.

For most of your intellectual property rights, think of a spectrum of possibilities for what you might do with them. This spectrum starts with full exclusion on one end. That's the sword-and-shield mode. In the middle is limited exclusion, where you let some people use your intellectual property for some purposes. That's the licensing approach. And then there's open access on the other end of the spectrum, where you permit unlimited use by others.

Limited Exclusion: The Revenue Stream

The intermediate option—limited exclusion—enables others to use your intellectual property on a limited basis to, for instance, generate revenues, extend your brand, or build your core market position through a network effect.

The primary reason to pursue a limited exclusion model is to make money in the near term from your intellectual property assets. The visible money in intellectual property is in the licensing business. Organizations that build major intellectual property portfolios and take licensing seriously can generate many millions or even billions of dollars per year in free cash flow by licensing intellectual property to one or more parties. Sometimes organizations even license their intellectual property to dread competitors—and profit handsomely from doing so. Notably, Intel and Advanced Micro Devices have long cross-licensed their intellectual property in their competitive pursuit to develop ever-faster processors.[1] Intel has also engaged in important cross-licensing agreements with NVIDIA, another of Intel's main competitors.[2]

Licensing is big business in a wide range of industries. There are two major categories of intellectual property licensing. The first major category in licensing is patents. The market for patent licensing is enormous, in fields such as computing, telecommunications, and the life and health sciences. The other category is the licensing of trademarks and copyrighted material for the purpose of merchandising. Typical examples include major brand names like Coca-Cola, sports leagues such as Major League Baseball or European League Football, and character and entertainment licenses like Disney's Hannah Montana.

Patent Licensing
Many of the biggest players in patent licensing are in IT and the life sciences. Some of the most eye-popping numbers come from the computer industry. Oracle, Microsoft, Symantec, and IBM have each earned a billion dollars or more in given years.

Table 6.1 Computer software

Oracle	$7.4 billion
Microsoft	$5.93 billion (likely higher)
Symantec	$1.31 billion
IBM	$368 million (in some years, much higher)

The chemical, pharmaceutical, and telecommunication industries each produce similarly remarkable returns from intellectual property licensing. Merck, Eli Lilly, Abbott Laboratories, and Johnson & Johnson, for instance, also generate substantial intellectual property revenues. Other leaders in these fields include:

Table 6.2 Chemical

DuPont	$1.076 billion
Dow Chemical	$247 million
PPG Industries	$48 million
Huntsman	$31.7 million

Table 6.3 Pharmaceutical

Wyeth	$383 million
Pfizer	$224 million
Bristol-Myers Squibb	$155 million

Table 6.4 Telecommunication

Comcast	$473 million
AT&T	$409 million
Verizon/Cellco	$47 million

Trademark and Copyright Licensing

But companies are not the only ones that develop technologies in the intellectual property business. Companies in the apparel industry, too, make millions per year by licensing their intellectual property—for example, designs and trademarks—to other organizations. Nike and VF Corporation, which owns the Wrangler and Lee jeans brands, are likely among the biggest licensors. Other organizations that generate impressive returns through licensing include:

Table 6.5 Apparel

Levi Strauss	$94.8 million
Jones Apparel Group	$52 million
Liz Claiborne	$41 million
Guess	$9.73 million

In the beverage business, Coca-Cola earns revenue by licensing its more than 450 brands to other organizations. Pepsi and Anheuser-Busch do the same thing. Molson Coors makes much of its intellectual property revenues through an "own-branding" strategy. In the food business, Pepsi is again a leader, along with Kraft Foods, Sara Lee, General Mills, and others.

And entertainment companies—content-based industries—are also enormous licensing machines.

Table 6.6 Entertainment

CBS	$1.3 billion
Viacom	$1.2 billion
Walt Disney	$750 million (approx.)
Time Warner	$722 million

In licensing, you have an almost-limitless range of options for how to structure deals and charge for the use of your intellectual property. A common strategy involves extensive price discrimination. As a patent licensor, for instance, you are likely to charge different rates to different consumers in different settings. Your pricing may vary based on what the organization is likely to do with your intellectual property, how badly they need it, what geographic region they are using it in, and so forth.[3] Within the pharmaceutical industry, it is common to set different prices based on geography—in other words, to define a market in geographic terms where the licensed intellectual property may be exploited or charge differential prices for a finished product based on where it is sold.[4] Computer organizations often make equipment that works more or less effectively based on what the consumer will pay; consider the IBM LaserJet printer Series E that was cheaper because it had the "extra" functionality of a chip that introduced delay, such that it printed only five sheets per minute instead of ten.[5] Price discrimination of this sort may involve some risk of annoying those who paid more for the same product or rights as others, but it also can result in an optimized revenue strategy if done right.

Companies that fail as operating businesses, too, can generate profits even after they have ceased making products. In the 1990s, despite brilliant minds and a lot of hype, Thinking Machines did not make it as a high-end computer manufacturer. But turnaround CEO Richard Fishman, brought in after the company had nearly failed, spun out T.M. Patents. This offshoot ended up generating hundreds of millions of dollars for shareholders by licensing the organization's technology to erstwhile competitors. Even if you are not going out of business, the exploitation of intellectual property assets is an increasingly common strategic move in lean times, as companies seek to shore up revenues.[6]

The notion of limited exclusion can also help by encouraging others to do something with your technology that you want them to do, but for which you don't require payment. In the computing industry, the developer of the most popular platform or programming language stands to benefit from the work of others. The epic battles between Microsoft, Sun, Novell, and others in the 1990s and into the twenty-first century demonstrate the many ways to profit from intellectual property. Each company has adjusted its strategy along the way; each continues to innovate in these ways today, as they compete aggressively in the sales process against one another.

Four graduate students founded Sun Microsystems in 1982 to develop computer workstations. From its inception, Sun embraced open systems. Its strategy involved publishing its own specifications and protocols to encourage others to create complementary products. Sun gained substantial a market share through the 1980s and 1990s in the enterprise computing business as a result.

Microsoft, founded in 1975 by Bill Gates and his high school friend Paul Allen, began as a software organization to serve computer developers. Microsoft soon became the dominant provider of operating systems for personal computers and applications for business use. Its strategy with respect to intellectual property started in a proprietary mode: Microsoft tended to develop its own software or buy code from others.

Sun and Microsoft have often been positioned as opposite one another in terms of their intellectual property strategy. Sun is frequently described, quite rightly, as a longtime supporter of open-source technologies and open standards in software. Microsoft was once pegged as a bête noire of the software industry because of its historically proprietary stance on intellectual property.

But on one level, the strategies of Sun and Microsoft to develop their enormously profitable, and usually competing, business lines are more similar than they are different. Both companies realized that they needed to let others connect to their systems in order to succeed. It is certainly true that Sun adopted a more open approach to the software community, while Microsoft long resisted aspects of the open-source and open-standards movements. Consider that a key aspect of the Microsoft strategy was to enable the applications of other companies to run in Microsoft's Windows operating system. Think of the many software packages that one runs regularly on a Windows PC that Microsoft did not make: Intuit's TurboTax, Apple's iTunes, Mozilla's Firefox Web browser, and so forth.

In functional terms, both the Sun and Microsoft intellectual property strategies over the past few decades are examples of limited exclusion, where the purpose was to let others have certain access to the code base in order to make systems that could interoperate. A recent agreement between Microsoft and Novell—long archenemies in the sales process—establishes a means for developers from the two companies to work together to make their systems more interoperable. A crucial part of this agreement is a covenant not to sue the other organization for intellectual property violations in the process.

The dynamic environment of Web 2.0—the social web that has emerged online—provides rich examples of the limited exclusion strategy. One of the keys to the explosive growth of Facebook has been its openness to other organizations developing applications that can work in Facebook's online environment. These "Facebook apps," similar to the development of iPhone and iPad applications, themselves have generated a mini-industry complete with venture organizations devoted to investing in companies that build them and advertising networks that seek to profit from them. Google, Yahoo!, Amazon, and other online giants have opened their systems to allow other organizations to use data and code that they have developed to create interoperable systems.

Each of these systems is backed up by a series of legal agreements. In Sun's case, for instance, it licensed its widespread Java technology to anyone who wanted to use it under a special license—the 1998 Community Source License. The most prominent open-source license is the GNU Public License, popularized by Richard Stallman and his Free Software Foundation. Facebook offers access to its systems under its own separate license, as do other Web 2.0 companies. The process of codeveloping software standards has a similar quality: companies are required to declare and check their rights at the door, agreeing to cooperate on certain terms together to develop a common standard for a given purpose.

In each of these cases, the goal is to create an ecosystem around your product or a system of value to multiple parties. There is an endless variety to the kinds of limited exclusion strategies that you might pursue, depending on the context. The underlying principle is simple: sometimes it makes sense to let others have limited access to your intellectual property in order to benefit in other ways over time.

Consider one further case that makes a strong argument in favor of limited exclusion. In the agribusiness world, in 1974, Monsanto came up with the blockbuster

The underlying principle is simple: sometimes it makes sense to let others have limited access to your intellectual property in order to benefit in other ways over time.

product Roundup, which enables farmers to kill weeds effectively. The product has sold well for decades. But Monsanto has in fact made more money on the intellectual property that it developed as it sought to build on its Roundup success. Monsanto engineers invented a product that made crops—the ones that the farmers wanted to grow and sell, like soybeans—immune to Roundup. The resulting invention, Roundup Ready, used a parasitic micro-organism known as Agrobacterium tumefaciens to create genetically modified soybeans. The company then made a key decision: instead of making the seeds available only through the company's own seed companies, it decided "to broadly license" the technology to other companies. As of 2009, 91 percent of the soybeans planted in the United States were genetically modified, of which 92 percent contained Monsanto's Roundup Ready trait. By the early 2000s, the sales of Roundup Ready through this licensing strategy eclipsed those of Roundup itself.[7]

A central argument about strategy in this book is that limited exclusion, not full exclusion, should be the starting point in your analysis. There is likely more to be gained by licensing some of your rights to others than there is to keeping it all to yourself (the sword-and-shield approach). And where it makes sense, giving it all away (the pure open-access approach) may also surprise you with its ability to provide greater longer-term advantage than exclusion-oriented strategies.

Full Exclusion: The Sword and the Shield

With full exclusion, you decide to exclude everyone else from using some or all of your intellectual property, and exploit it yourself to the greatest extent allowable under law. Sometimes this approach makes perfect sense. Let me start with the conventional wisdom about intellectual property as a sword and a shield, and then go from there.

In using intellectual property as a sword, you are assertively enforcing your own intellectual property rights against a competitor. This enforcement may take multiple forms. You might send the infringing party a letter that tells them to cease and desist from using your intellectual property. When they call you back, you enter into a licensing agreement that allows them to continue, but requires them to pay you and follow certain guidelines in their usage. That's what many organizations are after when they send the letter—a revenue stream, not a protracted lawsuit.

Perhaps, after you send the letter, you find that they don't call you back. They continue to violate your rights. Or more likely, you talk in guarded terms for a while about what a license might look like, but cannot agree to terms for a license. You decide to spend the money required to take them to court. Generally, they countersue you for something at the same time.

Intellectual property litigation has become a major field of law as a result of this practice. Some of the brightest lawyers in the world try these cases. Intellectual property litigation involving patent disputes often involves hundreds of millions or billions of dollars in disputed profits. Intellectual property litigation can drag on for many years, sometimes bringing down the organizations involved along with it. The costs of the legal fees involved are frequently in the millions of dollars. As two authors put it, "An average patent case will cost between $3 million and $10 million, and take two to three years to litigate" in the United States. And as an empirical study has shown, 75.6 percent of accused patent infringers ultimately win against those seeking to enforce patents through litigation.[8]

Few organizations wish to enter into intellectual property litigation if they can help it. That's not to say that it never makes sense. Sometimes it is the only way to stop another organization from infringing on your rights—in this way, the sword and the shield are effectively doing the same thing. And of course winners, using intellectual property as a sword, can come out much richer than they went in. The net effect, if you are successful, is either to block your competitor from copying what you have done or at least make them pay you for doing so. You often end up with a license agreement to govern the future usage of the intellectual property.

As a shield, you might use your intellectual property portfolio to block others from suing you for infringing on their intellectual property. The notion is a little bit like détente in the nuclear arms business. During the cold war, both the United States and the Soviet Union established huge arsenals of nuclear weapons. At a certain point, one of them wondered: Why do we need any more nuclear weapons? A possible theory was to ensure that the other side would never fire the first weapon, since they would then be assured of wiping one another out—or what's known as mutually assured destruction.[9]

The same theory holds for some organizations with respect to patents. If IBM and Microsoft ever got into disputes over patents, it almost certainly would become clear that each party—dread competitor of the other—was violating many of the other organization's patents. The effect would be massive claims against the other side. As a result, these titans rarely tangle over their intellectual property rights.[10]

You don't have to be as big as Microsoft and IBM to use your intellectual property as a shield in this way, however. You might imagine a scenario in which a competitor sues you for an intellectual property infringement. You respond with a notice that they are in fact violating your separate intellectual property rights. The net effect is not a huge penalty paid through a court decision but rather a cross-license between your two organizations—effectively canceling out the two infringing acts.

A few limitations to the sword-and-shield strategy are worth noting here. Intellectual property protections tend not to block big breakthrough innovations. Your use of intellectual property as a sword and a shield can be effective in blocking follow-on innovation by your competitors, where their new product or service is similar, but slightly different, from what you have done. You are not going to be able to block someone from coming up with a radically better drug, computer algorithm, or mousetrap. That particular battle has to be won in the research and development labs, not in the courtroom.

There are also legal limits concerning the extent to which you can rely on intellectual property as a sword and a shield. Put another way, there are limitations on the degree to which you can exclude others fully from using your intellectual property. The government will sometimes force you to license to others (compulsory licensing). In 2001, the US government (in)famously used the threat of compulsory licensing to authorize imports of generic ciprofloxacin for stockpiles against a possible anthrax attack.[11] In 2005, the US Department of Justice cited its right to use patents under compulsory licenses when it opposed injunctive relief for patent infringements relating to the BlackBerry email services supplied to both the government and private organizations that used the BlackBerry device to communicate with the government.[12] In other cases, the public has rights to use your intellectual property in limited ways (under the fair use doctrine in copyright, for instance, which allows for social commentary, among other socially desirable things). And if you succeed too wildly, you may even bump up against antitrust concerns—but that's a problem for another day.

The premise of this book is not that as a client, you should tell your lawyer never to sue a competitor to enforce your intellectual property. It is not to say that the courts in the eastern district of Texas, where many of these claims are brought, or the Court of Appeals for the Federal Circuit, where appeals of these claims end up, ought to shut their doors to litigants. The idea is instead simply to highlight the range of other, less costly and more collaborative options that an organization has in managing its intellectual property as well as creating long-term value in competitive ways.

Open Access: The Loss Leader

The open-access strategy falls at the other end of the spectrum from full exclusion. Sometimes it can make sense to give away certain forms of intellectual property in part or altogether. This strategy is a close cousin of the limited exclusion strategy, of course; the rationale is similar in that you are deciding to let other people use your intellectual property even if the law would allow you to prevent it. What's different in the open-access context is that you may find it makes sense to give away use of your intellectual property even if you aren't paid for the privilege.

The best example of this strategy is the extraordinary field of open-source software. Many other books have told this story well, so I will just offer the core idea here. In many instances, businesses, nonprofits, and individuals choose to create software, and then contribute their creations (which they otherwise could copyright or possibly patent) back to the public. This open-source software model has produced every imaginable type of computer code—some of it the most important code in a given domain. The Linux operating system, Apache Web servers, Mozilla Firefox Web browser, OpenOffice word processing software, and many other open-source projects have hundreds of millions of users between them, and are some of the best programs available.

In the open-source model, the creator generally does not give away all the rights free and clear to their creations. Under most open-source licenses, the creator puts their work into the public commons subject to a license that requires those who make use of the code to do the same. In other words, those who take the free software must give it away just as freely to others. As the open-source software leaders like to say, free software is free as in "free speech," not free as in "free beer."

As the open-source software example shows, there are sometimes strong reasons to let others use your intellectual property with fewer restrictions than the law establishes on your behalf automatically. It is possible to give away certain rights in certain creative works, as the Creative Commons model shows. Hundreds of millions of creative works have been licensed generally to the public under "some rights reserved" terms. Under the Creative Commons licenses, those who make works that are protected under copyright in turn give their works away to others according to the terms of a range of possible licenses. For instance, one such license says that someone may reuse your photograph as long as the user gives you credit or attribution. Another license is similar to the dominant free software licenses, which require those who use the work to "share alike" with others who might come after them.

Some pharmaceutical companies choose to freely license their drugs in order to spur work relevant to developing countries. GlaxoSmithKline recently created a "patent pool" of eight hundred granted or pending patents that researchers can license freely in order to develop and produce new products and formulations to combat neglected tropical diseases in least developed countries.[13] Not only does this generate public goodwill for GlaxoSmithKline but it also helps generate a network of potential collaborators with whom the corporation can license IP for profit.[14]

The important idea is to experiment within a given organization with different models for building and exploiting your intellectual property portfolio. The global knowledge economy calls for flexibility in intellectual property strategy. This flexibility can take many forms with respect to how you acquire, manage, and use your intellectual property, and how you work with others with respect to their intellectual property.

THE SPECIAL CASE
OF THE NONPROFIT

While this book has been written for the senior managers of any type of organization, most of the examples come from the business context. Businesses have tended to think more about their intellectual property than nonprofits have in the past. It's a mistake for most nonprofits to ignore intellectual property strategy. This chapter takes up some of the special circumstances that relate to nonprofits that may not apply in the context of business organizations. The primary difference is that the intellectual property strategies of openness may help nonprofits achieve aspects of their mission such as the broad dissemination of knowledge that are less important to businesses.

There are more similarities than differences in the strategic approaches that businesses and nonprofits should take to intellectual property. Both types of organizations have brands to consider; hire and manage personnel who create intellectual property; and need revenues to continue operating. In these respects and many others, most organizations share a series of traits that are relevant to intellectual property strategy.

The primary difference that I'll focus on here between businesses and nonprofits has to do with their respective missions. Most businesses, by law, need to focus largely on generating returns for their shareholders. They have a lot of latitude in terms of how they go about it, but they are primarily established for the purpose of maximizing profitability. To a large extent, they in fact have a legal obligation to focus on profitability rather than on other ancillary goals. Not so for nonprofits, which are set up to achieve a greater range of goals. These goals may include generating revenues to sustain operations, but also tend to include intangibles like creating and spreading knowledge, improving public awareness of a cause, bringing about social change, curing disease, and so forth. This difference in orientation opens up new possibilities for nonprofits that may not exist for all for-profits. This complexity can make the job of intellectual property strategy more important, not less so, and makes the need for creativity in this respect even greater.

The easiest case to make for the significance of an intellectual property strategy is for nonprofits in the knowledge-disseminating field. As in the case of for-profits, though, this is not the only type of nonprofit that can benefit. Nonprofits that have the most obvious need for an effective intellectual property strategy include universities, museums, libraries, and public media organizations. These institutions are akin to the media companies, software firms, and biotechnology entities that have such strong interests in intellectual property in the for-profit context.

Each of these knowledge-disseminating institutions is in an information business at core. These types of institutions are devoted to one or more parts of the process of creating, curating, distributing, and preserving various forms of ideas, expression, and knowledge. Their goals may be accomplished through a broad range of activities related to intellectual property. They may succeed by creating intellectual property, setting it in the context of other information such as metadata, sharing it with the public, and preserving it for the long term.

Let me start with one of the clear cases, where it is plain that intellectual property interests are relevant to the institution at a core level. Consider the interests of a major library. This library holds materials that are intended, as a matter of the library's mission, to be made available to the public, but that are not held by anyone else. This scenario applies equally to the New York Public Library, the Bodleian Library at Oxford University, the ancient abbey library in the heart of St. Gallen, Switzerland, the religious libraries of East Asia that hold ancient writings, and thousands of other libraries around the world. In

Each of these knowledge-disseminating institutions is in an information business at core. These types of institutions are devoted to one or more parts of the process of creating, curating, distributing, and preserving various forms of ideas, expression, and knowledge. Their goals

may be accomplished
through a broad range
of activities related
to intellectual property.
They may succeed
by creating intellectual
property, setting it in the
context of other infor-
mation such as meta-
data, sharing it with the
public, and preserving
it for the long term.

each case, they hold intellectual property in the form of materials that are unique.

The question for each of these libraries is what to do with the intellectual property in their possession. Some of the time, the materials are held in copyright by someone else, such as the author or publisher of a recently published book. In that case, the choice is made clear through the law: the library may acquire, catalog, contextualize, reference, and lend the work in various ways, but not much else. Yet what about a rare or even unique ancient manuscript to which copyright no longer applies?

The library has a few choices. One option is to do nothing in particular. This ancient manuscript is kept in a climate-controlled environment. Its value has been assessed at over a hundred thousand dollars if it were sold in an auction. It may or may not have been insured. When a patron comes to ask for it, the library can decide whether or not to bring the manuscript out and let them look at it, or can keep it locked up.

In the digital era, the library's options have grown. A new option is to invest in the digitization of the manuscript. By using an elaborate system of cameras and cradles, a valuable manuscript can be digitized without much risk to the material itself. The digital version could be used as a backup in case the original is harmed, stolen, or lost to fire. Or the digital version could be the one that is shared with researchers when they come to do their work on the document instead of the original one, which can be fragile.

The library has a few additional options related to the digitization of the work. In the real world, libraries have tight budgets and cannot afford to digitize everything they have the right to digitize. Let's imagine that this library does not have the money to digitize this manuscript and others like it over the course of the coming decade, but they would like to do so. The library could partner with a for-profit publisher. The publisher might well pay to digitize the collection of works, subject to a contract that would let the publisher sell the digital files to other libraries for a limited period of time—say, five years. For every sale, the library would receive a cut of the royalties paid by the other libraries to the publisher. At the end of the contract term, the library would get the digital scans of the works back, free and clear.

In this licensing example, most parties involved clearly benefit. The library with the manuscript gets to have it scanned sooner than it otherwise would have and also benefits from a modest stream of royalty revenues. The publisher or publishers who license the works get access to materials to sell to other libraries as part of their digital collections that they otherwise would not be able to sell. The other libraries that pay for the publisher's digital collections can then make the manuscripts available to their patrons, who now do not have to fly to the first library to view them (with the corresponding benefits to the environment for the carbon not emitted).

Why might this strategy not be sound? One argument is that the public at large could be harmed by this approach. If the library were simply to digitize the manuscript on its own and put it on the Web, the contention goes, then the public at large would have had access to the knowledge earlier than under the library-publisher partnership model. That may be true, but it is not practical; libraries today, facing consistent budget cuts, are forced to reduce services, not to increase them. Where funds are constrained, this type of library-publisher agreement serves the public better and more quickly than waiting for library budgets to improve. Alternately, if a library enters into an exclusive license with one publisher rather than licensing broadly, competing publishers might be harmed by the exclusive deal, or perhaps the public broadly would be harmed indirectly through the lack of competition. But in most cases, these potential harms are outweighed by the many public benefits of this type of licensing arrangement.

The library then faces another choice at the end of the five-year term. With the scan of the original manuscripts now in hand, should the library put it on the Web for anyone to see, perhaps contextualized as part of a fabulous online collection, or should the library keep the scan close at hand? Or should it seek another publisher who might wish to exploit the works in a new, profit-oriented fashion, in a manner that would generate further funds for the organization? Taking up the problem, the board of this particular library might consider whether the benefit of making the knowledge broadly and freely available is more important to its mission than keeping the collection of that library accessible only to a limited set of patrons who can come to the physical location. In a future version of libraries, the special and historical collections along with the range of services offered, as opposed to the general collections that are broadly available, may be what sets libraries apart from one another.

The same general problem faces museums, universities, and public media organizations. Replace the ancient manuscripts with digital images of works of art, and the analysis is not dissimilar. The same is true for universities and certain teaching materials. If one could choose whether to keep a series of lectures only for fee-paying students, or make the videos freely available on YouTube or iTunes University, which makes more sense for the institution? If a podcast series can reach more users online, and draw people back to a public media outlet's Web site or channel, doesn't it make sense to offer them freely online to the world? There are wrinkles, but the core considerations are similar. Cultural institutions have to look hard at their missions, and ask what ends are served by the distribution in various ways of rare or unique materials and information, whether their own work products or the holdings in their collections.

The movement toward open access to scholarly publications is another example of this same puzzle that is facing every major university in the world. Many parts of Harvard and MIT, for instance, have declared a policy of making their faculty's scholarly journal articles freely available online. For most faculty members of universities, our goal is not to generate profit from our scholarship; instead, our goals are the dissemination and growth of knowledge, and perhaps increased fame for the author and their employer. Given that open-access publishing is likely to increase the number of potential readers and improve the likelihood of an article being cited by another author who comes along later, the choice to publish on this basis can be clear for many faculty members.

Open-access policies are not without controversy, on campuses and beyond. Most universities have not yet adopted such approaches, though the number is growing each year. Opponents argue that scholarly societies and university presses as well as for-profit publishers will be hurt by the decreased publication sales for journals where the work is to be made freely available online. Publishers assert that the profits they will be able to generate in an open-access world will decrease, which in turn will diminish the editorial and marketing support they can provide to scholars seeking to publish their work. Others may fear that the university experience itself may be devalued by sharing unique scholarly materials online. MIT, however, which has made not just scholarly articles but also much of its teaching material available online through its Open CourseWare initiative, seems to have benefited from the positive glow of its decisions and the greater reach of its community's intellectual property, not the other way around.

Universities also face a variant of this conundrum when it comes to the licensing of their scientific advancements. Big research universities tend to enter into exclusive licenses with corporate partners to bring their faculty members' scientific innovations to market. These deals can generate large amounts in revenues for the universities involved: consider the deal between Gilead Sciences and Royalty Pharma, which paid Emory University $525 million in cash for use of the drug emtricitabine, also known as Emtriva.[1] Such deals, when made on an exclusive basis, may well be the best way to extract the largest cash payments for the universities involved. As an alternative approach, some universities might consider entering into nonexclusive arrangements that allow a greater range of private firms to innovate using universities' intellectual property, perhaps with lower royalty rates in total. The net cash proceeds to universities might be lower in the nonexclusive context than in the exclusive one, but the benefit to society may be greater. It is utterly conceivable that a more open approach to intellectual property licensing could lead to better research, on campus and off, if the ability to make use of the scientific advancements were more broadly and openly licensed. Universities compete fiercely for top research talent, just as for-profit corporations do. Universities might gain a leg up in the expensive and competitive labor market for researchers if they were able to attract faculty members interested in this open-licensing approach. The leadership at universities ought to weigh these various, potentially competing values in setting a general approach to intellectual property agreements.

Foundations face a similar series of choices with respect to intellectual property. In the context of federal grant making, the US government often requires grantees to make the benefits of federally funded research available broadly on an open-access basis. Increasingly, private foundations are thinking about their role in the dissemination of the research that they underwrite. Foundation executives are beginning to consider the way in which an insistence on open-licensing policies—based, for instance, on the Creative Commons model—may further their core missions.[2]

Many universities, libraries, museums, foundations, and public media organizations presented with these types of choices are deciding to share the information broadly online, rather than keeping information close at hand to generate a competitive advantage. If the default in the for-profit world is to generate maximum revenues from the licensing of intellectual property, the default in the non-profit setting is probably to make intellectual property as broadly available as possible. This general inclination toward openness on the part of knowledge-disseminating nonprofits versus maintaining proprietary control is a good thing for society at large.

The notion of a broad as well as increasing range of options for how to manage and exploit intellectual property holds true in the nonprofit context as it does in the for-profit world.

Universities, libraries, museums, and many other non-profit organizations can learn from the intellectual property practices of businesses, too. There may be cases, as in the for-profit context, where the optimal strategy for the nonprofit institution is to stick with profit maximization—to emphasize the licensing-for-cash option when it comes to intellectual property usage. In generating this extra cash flow, your nonprofit institution may be better positioned to meet your core goals in other ways. In this sense, intellectual property may be more important as a cash cow than as something to disseminate.

The fundamental idea of this book—that all types of organizations have an intellectual property portfolio and ought to have an intellectual property strategy—is equally true of nonprofits as it is of for-profits. Return to the analysis in earlier chapters and apply the same tools to the nonprofit context. The simplest point to recognize is that all organizations, whether or not in the knowledge-dissemination business, potentially hold valuable trademarks in their names and the symbols that describe them. In the case of nonprofits, these brands often bear significant goodwill, generated through their success in driving a public-spirited mission over time. Think of the positive things that one associates with the American Red Cross, Sierra Club, Ford Foundation, or National Association for the Advancement of Colored People. This "brand-name value" of well-known institutions itself has value that can be captured in myriad ways—such as through financial arrangements—that may help you accomplish your goals. A licensing arrangement that involves the use of a nonprofit's name, for instance, might be enormously valuable in raising awareness for a cause—a crucial goal for your organization—rather than as a direct revenue-generating matter.

These examples from the nonprofit context, repeated every day in the digital era, demonstrate how the choice of what to do with an institution's intellectual property is rarely straightforward. The outcome of these decisions ought to be governed by looking to the organization's mission and how it can be best served over time by various intellectual property strategies. A nonprofit might well decide that giving away intellectual property is the simplest, clearest way to serve its mission. But it is just as possible that a creative licensing arrangement—related to the trademark in its name or a famous character, as in the case of the CTW; copyrighted materials that it holds or underwrites, as in the case of a private foundation; or the patented inventions that its researchers dream up, as in the case of universities—could do as much, if not more, than a purely open strategy to advance the organization's mission through expanded reach, or the revenues that might come along with it. The choices that face a nonprofit in intellectual property strategy require much the same level of sophistication, and sometimes more, than in the for-profit context.

FUTURE OUTLOOK

The fast pace of change is one of the main characteristics of the intellectual property field. The single most important thing you can do as a CEO or senior manager is to ensure that your strategy is dynamic and forward-looking. Now that you have your asset class established with intellectual property, you are prepared to take advantage of changes in the field of intellectual property that will affect your industry.

Look to the Edges

A key to finding the right balance that you need to strike in your intellectual property strategy—and determining how your organization can benefit from intellectual property—is to look to the edges of the marketplace.

Edge 1: Places Where the Marketplace for Intellectual Property Is Changing Fast

Intellectual property is a field in flux. Though that's always been true to some extent, it has never been more critical than it is in today's increasingly global, knowledge-based economy. The manner in which your organization invests in the development of intellectual property, how you account for the intellectual property rights you hold, what you can do to exploit these rights, and the value placed on intellectual property by investors, acquirers, and partners are all changing rapidly.

First, while the market in intellectual property rights is growing, it is not mature—at least not on the patent side. Despite all the activity associated with the valuation of intellectual property assets and the hundreds of billions of dollars involved in licensing around the world, there's no established market for intellectual property licenses and asset sales. There is somewhat more stability in the marketplace for trademarks and copyrights for the purpose of merchandising, but even there, royalty rates can range from the low single digits up to more than 20 percent for the hottest properties.

At the moment, the market for intellectual property is a little bit like the one for local real estate: intellectual property is worth what someone else will pay for it. There's certainly no big, public market for intellectual property rights with many buyers. There is an asymmetry to this market that could work to your advantage if you are a sophisticated player.

Second, the legal and regulatory environment with respect to intellectual property, too, is unstable—no doubt a driver of the changing practices by organizations. Proposals to reform patent and copyright law, in particular, are on the front burners in the United States as well as key markets in Europe and Asia. The value to organizations of other areas of intellectual property—such as the diametrically opposed trade secrets (by definition, closely held) and trademarks (when valuable, widely disseminated)—continues to increase in significant ways. At stake is nothing short of the future of what it means to be an innovative organization and how to value your assets.

Two major patent reform efforts in the United States could dramatically change the landscape of intellectual property law along with what it means to business. The first is broad reform proposals for the patent system at large. The second relates to so-called follow-on biologics—especially important to the pharmaceutical industry. (As I've done throughout this book, I'm setting aside the question of what kind of change would be "good for society" as a matter of public policy.)

For the past several sessions in the US Congress, debate has swirled around the topic of systemic patent reform. From a lobbying perspective, large IT companies primarily drive the main proposals. Some lobbyists argue that the patent system is badly broken. Too many low-quality patents are issued, they say, by too few qualified patent examiners. The process takes too long, others say, and achieves a low-quality result. Some biotech and pharmaceutical companies complain that patent terms are not sufficiently long in order for organizations to recoup the costs associated with research and development of new drugs as well as Food and Drug Administration (FDA) trials. Others disagree just as adamantly: the system is working well enough, and changes will only benefit incumbents, who have all the patents they need today.

Most of these proposals hark back to a major study in 2004 by the National Academy of Sciences on the need to reform the patent system.[1] For the purposes of anticipating where things might go, one might look to the principles set forth in this report as likely to occur over time. The report calls for greater transparency in the patent system, increased public participation, and greater funding for the system at large.

The second major series of proposals focus on the issue of follow-on biologics—medicines that are similar to, but not the same as, innovator biologics. The powerful congressman Henry Waxman of California argues that we should make it much easier for innovation to occur on the basis of work previously done by other organizations. His proposals would allow the FDA to consider data generated by an innovator to establish the safety and efficacy of a follow-on biologic sharing structural and functional similarity to the innovator product, thus decreasing the cost and time needed to bring follow-on biologics to market. On the other hand, the big pharmaceutical organizations contend that this type of legislation would harm innovation by giving insufficient data exclusivity to the original developers of biologics.[2] On the flip side, this change would benefit the makers of generic drugs as well as significantly decrease the cost of biologics to consumers through increased competition. This series of possible changes would also affect the way that the FDA carries out its regulatory charge.

The courts are also involved in the process of changing intellectual property law. One important court-driven change, for instance, relates to the patentability of business methods. Under recent case law, it may be getting somewhat harder to patent a method in the United States.[3]

Third, intellectual property strategies are getting much more sophisticated. This is where the real opportunity lies for CEOs and senior managers. Organizations that figure out how to be creative in getting and using intellectual property are at a huge strategic advantage. Rather than seeing things as cut-and-dried, business leaders who are looking for new edges in intellectual property licensing and exploitation stand to benefit.

Edge 2: Changes in Social Norms

As every parent of a teenager knows, young people often relate to intellectual property very differently than did their parents and grandparents. There is no secret as to why Tower Records liquidated its stores or why Napster was so instantly popular when it hit the Internet scene. Young people love digital media. Many of them are creative in their reuse of copyrighted works, especially online. But many young people do not pay for the music and movies that they enjoy. This phenomenon is not limited to the United States or even only to young people.

Another aspect to social norms and intellectual property can be viewed through the lens of debates about patent reform, or the analogous debates about the relative merits of open-source and proprietary software. There is cultural force behind the idea of sharing software code, and then selling services and other applications of the code to customers—a concept at the core of the open-source software movement's success. Particularly in the online world of chat rooms, blogs, and other social media, these strong views of a vocal community are quickly visible. Think also of what it means that Wikipedia has become by far the largest encyclopedia in the world, created entirely by volunteers with no obvious profit motive. In fields like computing, it's crucial to pay attention to this community as well as consider the merits of its argument, even if it is not your core strategy to operate in an "open-source" mode.

These changing views of intellectual property amount to a trend that you need to watch, and it has a range of different implications. In one sense, it appears to be a challenge to the notion of thinking of your intellectual property as an asset class. If a generation of young people refuses to respect the intellectual property of others, the job of enforcing your intellectual property over time might seem to be a Sisyphean task. In some fields, this turns out to be true; ask the software executives leading companies in many parts of East Asia about piracy and you will see that they indeed have their hands full.

The more fundamental lesson from these changes in social norms is the need to be flexible and open to multiple strategies. Over time, these same young people who today are sharing the copyrighted music of others illegally are becoming creators themselves. They are going to work for companies in knowledge-based businesses. They will become the leaders helping to strike a balance between intellectual property protection and the legitimate interests of the public at large in ideas and expressions. As a business leader, you stand to benefit by listening to what these young people are really saying about their views on intellectual property as a guide to where the cultural and economic marketplace for intellectual property is heading.

Edge 3: International Dimensions to Intellectual Property

No discussion of intellectual property at this moment in history is complete without reference to its international dimensions. The global business network—comprised of connected marketplaces, human beings who travel back and forth, and information that flows over networked technologies—has already had dramatic implications for how intellectual property must be managed. The world's economies and cultures are increasingly interconnected. Intellectual property flows across national borders as well as markets in new and more profound ways than ever before.

It's instructive to consider the view from China. No one can say for sure whether a culture of intellectual property protection will arise over time. Will China be like the United States in changing its views when it becomes a net exporter of IP? Or is the cultural heritage so strong as to ensure a different outcome in future years?[4]

To listen to the government of China, the answer is fairly straightforward. The state is pursuing a national intellectual property strategy that includes the extension of rights in intellectual property and greater enforcement. In speeches delivered in China and at international forums like Davos, Prime Minister Wen Jiabao has repeatedly described the state's commitment to the development of a stronger, tighter regime of intellectual property protection over time. He has likewise stressed the extent to which the development of global markets for intellectual property is a crucial competitive element for any state in the coming decades.[5]

Some of the finest legal minds in China are considering this problem, in big law firms and at the best law schools. It's important to listen to what academics and practitioners in Beijing and Shanghai are saying about it. The mantra of "just increase enforcement" does not resonate. We in the United States can pound our chests about the need to enforce our rights as much as we like, and sometimes it will work—especially when linked to trade sanctions. But we cannot force another government, and particularly local provincial ones, to carry out the enforcement of laws that they don't consider a priority.

Russia provides a similar example to China. Intellectual property rights are less consistently enforced in Russia than they are in the United States. This difference plays out, for example, in the struggle to become the top online social network in Russia. The leading locally developed social network, Vkontakte, or VK.com, boasts seventy-five million members globally, primarily in Russia or among Russian speakers from other parts of the world. Much of the usage of VK relates to sharing media of interest with your friends. Often, these movies or songs are subject to copyright. Facebook, by contrast, has a policy of keeping copyrighted movies and music off the site. Though fast growing in Russia, Facebook has a big challenge in terms of competing with a locally developed firm that takes a less stringent view about intellectual property protection, consistent with local (though not all global) norms.

So what is to be done? One approach is to consider alternative modes to profiting from knowledge and information. Another is to push the sword-and-shield approach to its fullest extent: to continue to fight for the full enforcement of rights established in the United States or Europe. If you take this approach, it's crucial that you take a practical view: there will be leakage, at least for the foreseeable future, in China and other states that don't have the same background, culture, and legal system that we do. At a bare minimum, price this leakage into your models.

Edge 4: Work with—or Become—a Company That Helps to Solve IP Problems

One of the biggest hassles with respect to intellectual property is figuring out how best to enforce your rights in a global economy. In some parts of the world, piracy is more common than compliance in terms of intellectual property law, especially among consumers. Big companies like Microsoft devote a great deal of energy in the form of senior staff time to the task of increasing compliance with its intellectual property rights around the globe.

Even if you are not precisely in the business of creating intellectual property, you might consider ways to benefit from the problems associated with intellectual property creation, management, and enforcement. It stands to reason that as economies become increasingly knowledge based, the importance of intellectual property management as an asset class will take on greater significance. This pattern points to a burgeoning field. Consider the problems that I've raised in this book. Organizations need expert help in managing, enforcing, and even strategically sharing their intellectual property to take advantage of increasingly open marketplaces and interoperable business ecosystems.

There is also increasing legal pressure on companies to protect the intellectual property of others. This notion is called intermediary liability. YouTube, now a subsidiary of Google, has run into this problem in an expensive way. Holders of intellectual property have sued YouTube on the grounds that the video-sharing site has not done enough to protect the intellectual property rights of third parties. For instance, Viacom has sued YouTube because of the number of episodes from popular sites such as Comedy Central that have popped up online. Viacom, among other rights holders, criticizes what it considers YouTube's willful blindness to the copyright infringement happening on the video-sharing site. Viacom's lawyers want YouTube to take steps to police and limit the amount of infringing material hosted on the wildly popular site, but has failed—so far—to press its claims successfully in court.

There is a shortage of expertise in key areas of this field. One example of a type of business that stands to benefit from the growing importance of intellectual property

It stands to reason that as economies become increasingly knowledge based, the importance of intellectual property management as an asset class will take on greater significance.

is that of developing ways to detect when someone's intellectual property is being used online without permission and studying trends in piracy. Various companies are in this line of business. BayTSP helps organizations monitor the agreements they have with others for the monetization of intellectual property online. Attributor tracks content that you own as it is republished across the Web, serving organizations like the Associated Press. Affine offers a technology that can recognize your brand logo or the face of a celebrity as they appear in videos on social network sites. Each of these companies provides a service that helps intellectual property owners to monitor how others are using their content and, where appropriate, enforce their rights in the case of unlawful usage.

A more dramatic example is what Steve Jobs did with respect to the music recording industry. In crisis from changes wrought by the information economy, the recording industry was struggling to maintain its revenue sources and profitability after Napster and peer-to-peer file-sharing service became popular globally. Jobs—a computer guy—came up with the iPod and the iTunes Music Store as attractive, legal alternatives to stealing music. In effect, Jobs helped to create a huge and viable market for downloads of individual songs and albums. In the process, he also aided his own company to open up a series of new hit product lines, from the iPod to the iPhone and the iPad, built in no small part on the innovations that Apple brought to bear on the problem of digital music. Jobs built on the intellectual property of others and added his own genius to the mix. In helping to solve one big intellectual property problem—at least partially, anyway—Jobs created a new business ecosystem in which his own company would dominate for a decade or more. In fact, Apple now has one of the largest market capitalizations of any technology company in the world—and is one of the world's most valuable companies by any metric.[6]

A Double Bottom Line for Intellectual Property: Strike a Profitable Balance, and Be Ready to Change

The hardest challenge that the CEO or senior manager faces in terms of intellectual property strategy is balancing the natural desire for control against the opportunities as well as challenges afforded by openness. These strategies are often in tension—a tension that may be impossible to resolve in full. But the creative use of a range of strategies in different circumstances can help an organization in myriad ways. These strategies can generate near-term profits for your organization while positioning you for a dynamic information-based global marketplace.

Organizations have traditionally created value primarily through innovations within the organization. Your employees innovate, you then build a market around what they have created, and finally you defend that market. Today, that's still true to some extent. And it may well even serve as the cornerstone of your overall intellectual property strategy.

But it shouldn't be the sum total of your approach. It is increasingly the case that many relevant innovations are made by others. The most familiar example is innovation by academic laboratories in the life sciences, which are licensed and exploited by private organizations. The open-source movement in the software field (think of the software that runs most servers, for instance, which is built on open-source technology) is another familiar story. As we've seen, much of the Web 2.0 environment online runs on a combination of open-source software and an interoperable series of Open APIs. Today, in some industries, the most interesting innovators are the organization's competitors and customers. These are all instances where strategies that are not simply about full exclusion can reap huge benefits for organizations of all stripes.

The costs and benefits associated with intellectual property protection and litigation are growing over time, as organizations apply for far more patents each year in more markets and more industries. The quality of those patents, many critics argue, is low—and not getting better anytime soon. Likewise, entire industries are built online at the margins of the copyright law, where multibillion-dollar investments (think of Google's acquisition for $1.4 billion of YouTube, the most prominent Web-based distributor of video content) bring potentially crippling liability with them. Organizations stand to gain tremendously from the innovations of their customers or members of relevant communities, as the open-source movement has shown, if the CEO can determine how to be open to listening to and incorporating these suggestions.

It is essential to focus on the big picture. Organizations in most industries connect together to form an ecosystem. As the intellectual property business grows in size and reach, the impact of the innovation of one organization increasingly affects what another organization may do. An organization's competitors may innovate in ways that erect roadblocks to a CEO's progress in important markets. Sometimes the threat comes from a third party seeking to profit from intellectual property development directly. A tide of innovation—where organizations are cooperating in some contexts rather than only competing—frequently can lead to higher returns for all market participants along with better choices, lower prices, and greater benefits for consumers. Such systems of interoperability are often greased by the use of innovative intellectual property strategies.

What's missing in many organizations is a nuanced and coordinated view of this increasingly challenging topic.

The CEO or senior manager needs to ask their team these questions: What intellectual property assets are available to my organization, how can I secure and build on them, and how can they be monetized in a way that makes sense for the near and long term? The answers to each are almost certain to be dynamic—changing with each passing year. Your strategy, in turn, needs to be just as dynamic and forward thinking.

Fundamentally, business leaders need to recognize the fact that in our networked information age, it is not only sometimes hard to enforce scarcity when it comes to ideas and forms of expression but also not the best idea in all cases. Powerful forces—cultural views in other parts of the world, widespread social norms (good and bad), and certain real benefits to open-information environments—are making it hard for the full exclusion approach to work over time. Full exclusion has its place. But it is not tenable in all cases. And it's not always the best way to think about and exploit intellectual property. Organizations big and small—from Microsoft and Merck to start-ups around the world—are beginning to see it this way.

You already know that your organization needs to innovate in terms of how you develop products or services. If you take away one concept from this book, it's this: you *also* need innovate in the development of your intellectual property strategy. Your organization can benefit in the near term from flexible, dynamic intellectual property strategies while positioning itself for success in the growing, shifting global knowledge economy, but only if you take intellectual property strategy seriously and seek out opportunity at the edges of the economic system.

AFTERWORD
What the Author Really Thinks

Throughout this book, I've made an argument that is entirely practical. I think that it is right for organizations, whether non- or for-profit ones, to explore a range of intellectual property strategies because I believe it will help your organization achieve its own goals. I maintain that it's more often the case that open strategies are the right idea for the long term and that full exclusion strategies will work over time only in certain circumstances. At no point in this book have I sought to convince you based on my views of what is best for society at large. My approach has been to suppress my personal opinions of what type of public policy we ought to adopt in matters of intellectual property.

If you've made it this far, I figure that it is only fair to say what I really think about intellectual property policy, independent of what might be good as a strategic matter for a given organization. So here goes.

At the most basic level, my view is highly conventional: I favor a balance between the rights of creators and the public. This balance ought to be set in such a way as to serve a series of occasionally conflicting interests. It also should ensure that creators are given adequate incentive to create, which means that they ("we," I should say; I'm an author, for instance) are paid fairly for their work. Concurrently, this balance should be set in such a way as to ensure that the public has access to ideas and expression over time along with rights to make use of those ideas and expression in certain ways. Intellectual property policy should seek to promote innovation, fairness, and the public interest all at once.

To get one level more specific: I think our intellectual property law is today generally skewed too far in favor of creators and too little in favor of the public at large. There are a few areas where this skew is most apparent. I think the term for copyright in the United States is too long, especially after the Sonny Bono Copyright Term Extension Act. There is no need for a work to be subject to copyright for the author's life plus seventy years in order to promote creativity and ensure fair compensation for artists. As a second example, I believe that the patent system ought to be reformed to improve the quality of certain types of patents and ensure the broad dissemination of lifesaving drugs.

There is no need for a work to be subject to copyright for the author's life plus seventy years in order to promote creativity and ensure fair compensation for artists.

Outside the public policy context, I believe that institutions—non- and for-profit organizations—tend to serve the public interest when they pursue strategies of openness rather than exclusion. This bias no doubt colors the strategic advice that I give in the book's main text; it is for that reason that I point out the possibility of a conflict here. When a university makes its lectures or the works of its teachers broadly available online, people globally can benefit from this access to knowledge. When a public media outlet shares its documentaries and raw footage freely on the Web, we all benefit. When IBM or Microsoft engineers improve open-source code and contribute it to the commons, the world is better off. When generic drugs are sold at a low price to enable people suffering from AIDS to feel better or extend their lives, the benefits are obvious.

The business of intellectual property is about balance. The system needs to be calibrated such that there's sufficient incentive for creative people to innovate and effective marketers to disseminate innovative things. Just as an organization's approach to intellectual property ought to be about considering a range of options, so too should we think broadly and creatively about how the law of intellectual property evolves over time, in the public interest.

GLOSSARY

There are four primary types of intellectual property: copyright, patent, trademark, and trade secret.[1]

Copyright
A copyright involves exclusive rights given to the creator of an original, expressive work (literary, musical, dramatic, architectural, etc.) that allow the owner to reproduce, copy, distribute, perform, display, or sell their work. These rights are usually extended for a specific time period. They protect the form of expression, not the subject matter of the work. In the United States, these rights are automatically granted to the creator, though formal registration of copyrighted works can provide additional benefits to the copyright holder. These rights are constrained by a series of limitations and exceptions, such as the first-sale doctrine (which allows you as a customer or secondhand bookstore, for instance, to resell a used book) and fair use doctrine (which permits the creative reuse of copyrighted works in many cases, including allowing comedians to parody the works of others in certain circumstances, for example).

Patent
A patent gives a holder the legal right to prohibit others from using, making, selling, or importing a new and useful invention without permission. This invention may be in the form of an idea, or in some countries, a business method. A patent usually has a time limit and does not give the holder ownership rights (beyond the right to restrict others' use of the product) if the holder did not originally possess those rights.

Trademark
A trademark distinguishes a product from others in the marketplace and indicates its origin. Although a trademark can protect a wide range of modes of expression (words, phrases, or logos), it has to be distinctive and must represent something sold in the marketplace to receive federal protection in the United States. Trademarks ought to be registered with the US Patent and Trademark Office or similar offices around the world in order to be effectively licensed or defended.

Trade Secret

A trade secret is information a company utilizes in its business that is kept secret in the ordinary course of business to maintain the company's competitive advantage over competitors. It cannot be readily ascertainable by those who could profit from its disclosure and must derive independent economic value. Trade secrets can include formulas, patterns, processes, and devices. Google's search algorithm or Coca-Cola's formula are both examples of important trade secrets.

Other key terms used throughout the book are:

Character and Entertainment Merchandising

Character and entertainment merchandising involves the authorized use of the well-known personality features of a celebrity or fictional character in connection with the sale of goods or services. The primary goals of character or entertainment merchandising are to generate income for the owner of trademark and copyright interests in the original works as well as encourage customers to buy the product or service due to their affinity with the celebrity or character. The licensing of children's characters is a particularly strong area. Dora the Explorer, *Sesame Street* characters, Mickey Mouse, and others generate substantial income for the holders of the rights, and can help sell materials to young consumers and their parents. For nonprofits, licensing may also serve other crucial functions, such as funneling young people back to a Web site or program where they can gain educational benefits.

Court of Appeals for the Federal Circuit

In the United States, this special appellate court—also referred to as the "CAFC"—handles matters related to patent and trademark, among other specialty subjects. The Court of Appeals for the Federal Circuit is one of thirteen appellate courts and is located in Washington, DC.

Intellectual Property Audits

Intellectual property audits are evaluations of the merits, legal status, and value of a company's intellectual property assets. Audits help companies and other organizations determine what intellectual property assets they own, and discover current or potential legal problems or opportunities regarding their claims of ownership. An audit can also help a company determine if it has any unprotected assets, and from there, the necessary steps to protect these assets. Audits are useful for companies in the process of selling or acquiring property assets from a third party as well.

Intellectual Property License

An intellectual property license is an agreement through which an owner gives a licensee permission to use the owner's intellectual property (a patent, trademark, name, etc.) in connection with the licensee's product or service. The right may not be exclusive but it is usually granted for a finite time period, in a specified location and for a particular purpose.

Merchandise Licensing

Merchandising licensing entails an agreement through which the owner of a product (artwork, television program, book character, etc.) gives a company permission to manufacture items that use either the product or parts of it in exchange for compensation. The owner's item must be protected under trademark or copyright laws for the agreement to be valid.

Reasonable and Nondiscriminatory Licensing Terms

Reasonable and nondiscriminatory licensing is used during industry standard-setting procedures. It is a mechanism by which companies that hold patents that are essential for organizations to conform to standardization efforts agree to allow their intellectual property to be licensed by other participants at a reasonable fee.

Sports Licensing

Sports licensing refers to licensing agreements by famous athletes, professional sports organizations, and universities with companies to use their name, logo, or related entities for purposes such as selling merchandise. For instance, the large professional sports leagues—such as Major League Baseball and the National Football League in the United States, and professional soccer (football) associations around the world—reap large profits from the sale of merchandise with logos and other protected intellectual property printed on them. Major colleges and universities, especially those with prominent sports teams, similarly earn substantial returns from licensing.

Trademark and Brand Licensing

Trademark and brand licensing refers to a company licensing its name, logo, or brand to be used on products sold by another entity. This is a dynamic segment of the licensing industry at large.[2]

Trade-Related Aspects of Intellectual Property Rights (TRIPS)

The TRIPS agreement is the most comprehensive international treaty on intellectual property rights. Countries that have signed the TRIPS agreement commit to provide a minimum level of protection for other members' citizen's intellectual property rights. The treaty's purpose is to promote the effective protection of intellectual property rights, reduce obstructions to international rights, and ensure that a country's regulations do not restrict trade. The TRIPS agreement also provides a mechanism for addressing intellectual property disputes.

Chapter 1

1. Karen Raugust, *The Licensing Business Handbook*, 7th ed. (New York: EPM Communications, 2008), v.

2. Kamil Idris, *Intellectual Property: A Power Tool for Economic Growth* (Geneva: World Intellectual Property Organization, 2003), 34.

3. This book is not meant to serve as a primer on the intellectual property law itself, nor does it constitute legal advice, but I say a bit more about each of these types of intellectual property assets in the glossary. I suggest further readings at the end of the book for those who would like to go deeper in any of these areas. One of the best recent books of this sort is Steven J. Frank's *Intellectual Property for Managers and Investors* (New York: Cambridge University Press, 2006), which offers more detail on intellectual property law as such from the perspective of a practicing attorney. The best advice on the law itself is, ideally, your in-house or outside counsel, who should be a key ally in setting the organization's intellectual property strategy.

4. In conversation with the author, Boston, MA, June, 2001.

Chapter 2

1. Separately, Apple and Nokia have sued one another over IPs related to smart-phones. See, for example, Chris F. Lonegro, "The Sword and the Shield of Patent Protection: Nokia v. Apple/Apple v. Nokia," February 2, 2010, available at http://www.lexology.com/library/detail.aspx?g=b62e2e12-d0f3-4e6a-8bf7-ea 055b5c8606.

2. RIM had its own costly, high-profile run-in with a patent holder, NTP, Inc.

3. See In re Bilski, 545 F. 3d 943, 88 U.S.P.Q. 2d 1385 (Fed. Cir. 2008).

4. As one example, on the question of the effects of patents on innovation, see James Bessen and Michael J. Meurer, *Patent Failure: How Judges, Bureaucrats, and Lawyers Put Innovators at Risk* (Princeton, NJ: Princeton University Press, 2008)—for the strong form of the argument that patents do not purely lead to innovation based on what they claim is the first comprehensive empirical analysis of the patent system.

5. It is only fair that I declare my bias, which I describe in greater detail in chapter 9: I favor many of the reforms that would roll back extensions of the intellectual property protection regime, especially in the area of copyright doctrine.

I don't think, for instance, that copyright term extension is necessary to promote innovation and creativity (what author, after all, is thinking about their great-great-grandchildren when they decide whether or not to write?), and believe it comes with costs that are net negative for society. This normative bias leads me to ask questions about whether there are better ways to benefit from ideas and information than the pure exclusion strategy I refer to in the book. But here I strive to be objective and present options to you as I see them through the lens of a business adviser, much as a lawyer does for a client (though, of course, this book does not and cannot constitute legal advice).

6. Even for smaller matters, intellectual property litigation costs can be prohibitive, and companies may find themselves unable to enforce some of their rights. Take it from Kirsten Osolind, the CEO of a small Chicago marketing organization called re:invention, who became embroiled in a trademark dispute with another company. After spending fifteen thousand dollars for the first three months of legal assistance in her bid to enforce her trademark rights, she learned that it would cost at least another hundred thousand dollars to bring her case to court and declined to pursue the matter further. See Elaine Pofeldt, "Marking Your Territory," *Go Magazine*, 85–87, January 2010.

7. See David A. Vise, "Google Ends Its Dispute with Yahoo," *Washington Post*, August 10, 2004, available at http://www.washingtonpost.com/wp-dyn/articles/A52880-2004Aug9.html.

Chapter 3

1. Robert M. Solow, "A Contribution to the Theory of Economic Growth," *Quarterly Journal of Economics* 70, no. 1 (February 1956): 65–94, available at http://www.jstor.org/pss/1884513.

2. See http://hd.engadget.com/2009/02/04/samsung-hedges-its-bets-with-unipixels-tmos-display-technology.

3. "The 'Real' Story behind the Sirius/XM Merger," SeekingAlpha.com, July 11, 2008, available at http://seekingalpha.com/article/84518-the-real-story-behind-the-xm-sirius-merger.

4. For details of the Sirius-XM joint development agreement along with other examples, see J. Derek Mason, *Critical Issues in Joint Development Agreements* (Alexandria, VA: Oblon, Spivak, McClelland, Maier and Neustadt, May 28, 2008), available at http://www.oblon.com/sites/default/files/news/414_B_0.pdf.

5. See http://www.bp.com/genericarticle.do?categoryId=2012968&contentId=7055476.

6. US General Accounting Office, "Intellectual Property: Federal Agency Efforts in Transferring and Reporting New Technology," GAO-03-47, October 2002.

See also the National Aeronautics and Space Administration patents licensed at the Ocean Tomo auction in fall 2008 in Chicago.

7. See Andrew Toole, "Does Public Scientific Research Complement Industry R&D Investment? The Case of NIH-Supported Clinical Research and Pharmaceutical Industry R&D," Center for European Economic Research, ZEW discussion Ppaper (2005), abstract available at http://ideas.repc.org.

8. For examples of and information regarding federal technology-transfer programs, see National Institute of Standards and Technology, *U.S. Department of Commerce, Federal Laboratory Technology Transfer, Fiscal Year 2007: Summary Report to the President and Congress* (2009), available at http://www.nist.gov/tpo/index.cfm.

9. For information on how to take advantage of the federal government's vast technology portfolio, you can visit the Federal Laboratory Consortium for Technology Transfer's Web site, available at http://www.federallabs.org/home/faqs.

10. Alison Frankel, "The Dam Breaks: Intellectual Ventures Files Three Patent Infringement Complaints in Delaware," *American Lawyer*, December 8, 2010, available at http://www.law.com/jsp/tal/PubArticleTAL.jsp?id=1202475921457&slreturn=1&hbxlogin=1.

11. See Sarah Jones, "Luna Purchases Rival's Patents," *Roanoke Times*, December 30, 2009, available at http://www.roanoke.com/business/wb/231303.

12. See http://www.businessweek.com/2001/01_10/b3722001.htm.

13. In 2008, the average total pendency of a patent application was 32.3 months in the United States. This figure relates to the average time from the most recent filing date, so the true figure might be significantly higher. See http://ipwatchdog.com/2009/04/22/uspto-backlog-patent-pendency-out-of-control/id=2848.

14. See John Rivzi, "Single Letter Wrong in Medical Patent on Heart Surgery Solution Spells Disaster," Medical and Dental Advice Patenting blog, September 28, 2009, available at http://www.medicaldevicepatentattorneys.com/2009/09/articles/drafting-medical-technology-pa/single-letter-wrong-in-medical-patent-on-heart-surgury-solution-spells-disaster. See also *Central Admixture Pharmacy Services Inc. v. Advanced Cardiac Solutions, P.C.*, 482 F.3d 1347 (2007) and subsequent history.

Chapter 4

1. For IBM, see http://www.businessweek.com/magazine/content/06_32/b3996062.htm?chan=tc&campaign_id=rss_tech. For LEGO, see http://outside innovation.blogs.com/pseybold/2008/05/lego-celebrates.html;http://www.wired

.com/wired/archive/14.02/lego.html. For PETCO, see http://www.womma.org
/casestudy/examples/automate-word-of-mouth-marketing/petco-analyzes-prod
uct-reviews.

2. See http://developer.apple.com/iphone.

3. See http://www.livescribe.com/cgi-bin/WebObjects/LDApp.woa/wa/Devel
operOverviewPage.

4. See http://www.marketingpilgrim.com/2007/04/google-maps-to-mash-up-com
panies-suckers.html.

5. See Henry Chesbrough, *Open Innovation: The New Imperative for Creating
and Profiting from Technology* (Cambridge, MA: Harvard Business Press, 2003).

6. See Dyan Machan, "Inventors Wanted," *SmartMoney Magazine*, March
2009, 42.

7. See http://www.informationweek.com/news/showArticle.jhtml?articleID
=197000211.

8. See Mark Blaxhill and Ralph Eckhardt, *The Invisible Edge: Taking Your Strategy to the Next Level Using Intellectual Property* (New York: Portfolio, 2009), 151.

9. "InnoCentive: A Market for Ideas," *Economist*, September 17, 2009.

10. The Generic Pharmaceutical Association commissioned a study by IMS
Health, available at http://www.gphaonline.org/about-gpha/about-generics
/case/generics-providing-savings-americans. The study argues that the generic
pharmaceutical industry saved US consumers $734 billion over the course of
a decade, with a savings of $121 billion in the year 2008 alone. Other pharma-
ceutical companies contend that this study is misleading.

11. See chapter 7 below.

12. On the prize system, see William W. Fisher and Talha Syed, *Drugs, Law,
and the Health Crisis in the Developing World* (Stanford, CA: Stanford University Press forthcoming). On Equitable Access licenses, see Amy Kapczynski,
Samantha Chaifetz, Zachary Katz, and Yochai Benkler, "Assessing Global
Health Inequities: An Open Licensing Approach for University Innovations,"
20 *Berkeley Technology Law Journal* 1031 (2005).

13. See Jonathan D. Rockoff and Ron Winslow, "Merck to Develop Biotech
Generics," *Wall Street Journal*, December 10, 2008, B1.

14. Thomas Rogers and Andrew Szamosszegi, "Fair Use in the U.S. Economy:
Economic Contribution of Industries Relying on Fair Use" (Washington, DC:
Computer and Communications Industry Association, 2010), available at
http://www.ccianet.org.

Chapter 5

1. Professor Tim Wu of Columbia Law School refers to this notion as "tolerated use." It is also referred to as "permitted use." See Tim Wu, "Tolerated Use," *Columbia Journal of Law and the Arts* 31, no. 4 (summer 2008): 617.

2. Jennifer Delson, "Got a License for that Pinata?" *Los Angeles Times*, June 19, 2005, available at http://articles.latimes.com/2005/jun/19/local/me-pinata19.

3. See http://www.unhappybirthday.com.

4. See http://www.law.umkc.edu/faculty/projects/ftrials/communications /ASCAP.html.

5. See "China Real Time Report: Another Yahoo-Alibaba Spat," September 10, 2010, available at http://blogs.wsj.com. See also Erica Werner, "Yahoo Execs Defend Company's Role in Arrest of Chinese Journalist," Associated Press Newswires, November 6, 2007. See also Stephanie Kirchgaessner, "Yahoo CEO Repents over Chinese Dissident," November 6, 2007, available at http://www.ft.com.

6. See Ashley Seager, "Starbucks, the Coffee Beans, and the Copyright Row That Cost Ethiopia 47 m. GBP," *Guardian*, October 26, 2006, available at http://www.guardian.co.uk/world/2006/oct/26/usa.ethicalliving (note that the *Guardian* mistook trademark interests for copyrights in the title as well as the body of the article). See also the press release that Starbucks issued a month later as part of its damage control, "Talks between Starbucks and the Ethiopian Government Positive and Ongoing," November 30, 2006, available at http://news.starbucks.com/article_display.cfm?article_id=126.

Chapter 6

1. See "AMD Reports Fourth Quarter Results," January 21, 2010, available at http://www.amd.com/us/press-releases/Pages/q4-earnings-2010jan21.aspx. See also George Chidi, IDG News Service, May 04, 2001, "AMD and Intel Renew Cross-licensing Agreement," available at http://www.itworld.com/IDG 010504amd_intel.

2. See http://www.extremetech.com/article2/0,1558,1729927,00.asp.

3. See William W. Fisher III, "When Should We Permit Differential Pricing of Information?" *UCLA Law Review* 55, no. 1 (2007).

4. See Patricia M. Danzon and Michael F. Furukawa, "Prices and Availability of Pharmaceuticals: Evidence from Nine Countries," *Health Affairs* 22, no. 6 (2003): W521–W536, available at http://content.healthaffairs.org/cgi/content /full/hlthaff.w3.521v1/DC1.

5. See Hal R. Varian, "Versioning Information Goods" (1997), available at http://www.ischool.berkeley.edu/~hal/Papers/version.pdf.

6. See Rachel Keeler, "Sharper Focus on Intellectual Property," *Financial Times*, November 18, 2008, available at http://www.ft.com.

7. Roger Parloff, "Fortune 500 Series: Monsanto," Fortune, Inc., 2010, available at http://money.cnn.com/2010/05/06/news/companies/monsanto_patent .fortune/index.htm. Another element of this story is the dispute between Monsanto, DuPont, other agribusinesses, and the US Department of Justice over whether Monsanto is abusing its monopoly position in Roundup Ready.

8. Paul M. Janicke and Lilian Ren, "Who Wins Patent Infringement Cases?" American Intellectual Property Law Association Quarterly Journal 34, no. 1 (2006).

9. See Kenneth N. Cukier, "A Market for Ideas," Economist, October 20, 2005.

10. Nathan Myhrvold, formerly the chief technology office of Microsoft and now principal of large rights aggregator Intellectual Ventures, argues that software titans "infringe lots and get away with it. They have made deliberate decisions not to check patents. They're afraid in the long run they'd have to pay somebody." Quoted in Victoria Slind-Flor, "IV Moves from Myth to Reality," Intellectual Asset Management, August–September 2006, 33.

11. See http://www.cptech.org/ip/health/cl/cipro.

12. US Statement of Interest, NTP, INC., v. Research in Motion, Ltd., November 2005.

13. A patent pool is a voluntary arrangement where a group or groups agree to license identified classes of patents and/or classes of technology to third parties on predetermined standard conditions. See http://www.gsk.com/collabora tions/patentpool.htm.

14. Indeed, the patents are only freely available to the extent that the products created are used in least developed countries. If used elsewhere, a different type of license must be negotiated with GlaxoSmithKline.

Chapter 7

1. "Gilead Sciences and Royalty Pharma Announce $525 Million Agreement with Emory University to Purchase Royalty Interest for Emtricitabine," Emory University press release, July 18, 2005, available at http://www.emory.edu /news/Releases/emtri.

2. Consider the research project conducted by my colleagues at the Berkman Center for Internet and Society at Harvard University on the copyright licensing opportunities of private foundations, available at http://cyber.law.harvard .edu/publications/2009/Open_Content_Licensing_for_Foundations.

Chapter 8

1. National Research Council of the National Academies of Sciences, Committee on Intellectual Property Rights in the Knowledge-Based Economy, Board of Science, Technology, and Economic Policy, A Patent System for the

Twenty-first Century (2004), available at http://www.nap.edu/openbook.php ?isbn=0309089107.

2. See, for example, "Follow-on Biologics Bill Threatens Innovation by Weakening Patent Rights," Holman's Biotech IP Blog, June 28, 2009, available at http: //holmansbiotechipblog.blogspot.com/2009/06/follow-on-biologics-bill-threatens.html.

3. *KSR v. Teleflex*, 550 U.S. 398 (2007); In re Bilski, 545 F. 3d. 943, 88 U.S.P.Q. 2d 1385 (Fed. Cir. 2008).

4. William Alford, *To Steal a Book Is an Elegant Offense: Intellectual Property Law in Chinese Civilization* (Stanford, CA: Stanford University Press, 1997).

5. See the Web site on Chinese intellectual property law and policy, available at http://www.chinaipr.gov.cn. For instance, consider Prime Minister Jiabao's speech at the Davos meeting in September 2009, available at http://www .chinaipr.gov.cn/policyarticle/policy/speeches/200909/544678_1.html. For similar pronouncements, see Mark Blaxhill and Ralph Eckhardt, *The Invisible Edge: Taking Your Strategy to the Next Level Using Intellectual Property* (New York: Portfolio, 2009), 15.

6. See Miguel Helft and Ashlee Vance, "Apple Passes Microsoft as No. 1 in Tech," *New York Times*, May 26, 2010, available at http://www.nytimes.com. See also Associated Press, "Apple Dethrones Microsoft as the Biggest Tech Company in the World," *Huffington Post*, May 26, 2010, available at http://www.huffingtonpost .com/2010/05/26/apple-market-cap-surpasse_n_590854.html.

Glossary

1. These definitions are drawn from a combination of sources. For more information of the definitional variety, consider Bryan A. Garner, ed., *Black's Law Dictionary*, 9th ed. (Eagan, MN: West Group, 2004); Kinley and Lange, P.A., *Intellectual Property Law for Business Lawyers* (Eagan, MN: West Group, 2010); J. Thomas McCarthy, Roger E. Schechter, and David J. Franklyn, *McCarthy's Desk Encyclopedia of Intellectual Property*, 3rd ed. (Washington, DC: Bureau of National Affairs, 2004); and Karen Raugust and the editors of the Licensing Letter, *The Licensing Business Handbook* (New York: EPM Communications, 2007). Other good sources include the Web sites of the US Patent and Trademark Office, the US Copyright Office, the World Intellectual Property Organization, and the World Trade Organization.

2. For more on this topic in general, see the International Licensing Industry Merchandiser's Association, available at http://www.licensing.org/education.

RECOMMENDED READING

Books

Alford, William. *To Steal a Book Is an Elegant Offense: Intellectual Property Law in Chinese Civilization*. Stanford, CA: Stanford University Press, 1997.

Arena, Christopher M., and Eduardo M. Carreras. *The Business of Intellectual Property*. Oxford: Oxford University Press, 2008.

Battersby, Gregory J., and Charles W. Grimes. *Licensing Royalty Rates*. New York: Wolters Kluwer, 2009.

Benkler, Yochai. *The Wealth of Networks*. New Haven, CT: Yale University Press, 2006.

Bessen, James, and Michael J. Meurer. *Patent Failure: How Judges, Bureaucrats, and Lawyers Put Innovators at Risk*. Princeton, NJ: Princeton University Press, 2008.

Blaxill, Mark, and Ralph Eckardt. *The Invisible Edge: Taking Your Strategy to the Next Level Using Intellectual Property*. New York: Portfolio, 2009.

Chesborough, Thomas. *Open Innovation: The New Imperative for Creating and Profiting from Technology*. Cambridge, MA: Harvard Business Press, 2006.

Christensen, Clayton M. *The Innovator's Dilemma: When New Technologies Cause Great Organizations to Fail*. Cambridge, MA: Harvard Business School Press, 1997.

Correa, Carlos M., ed. *South Perspective: A Guide to Pharmaceutical Patents, Volumes 1 and 2*. South Centre, 2008. http://www.southcentre.org/index.php?option=com_content&task=view&id=678&Itemid=1.

Dobrusin, Eric M., and Ronald A. Krasnow. *Intellectual Property Culture: Strategies to Foster Successful Patent and Trade Secret Practices in Everyday Business*. Oxford: Oxford University Press, 2008.

Fisher, William W., III. *Promises to Keep: Technology, Law, and the Future of Entertainment*. Stanford, CA: Stanford University Press, 2004.

Glazier, Stephen C. *Patent Strategies for Business*. 3rd ed. New York: Leo Baeck Institute, 2000.

Goldstein, Paul. *Copyright's Highway: From Gutenberg to the Celestial Jukebox*. Rev. ed. Stanford, CA: Stanford Law and Politics, 2003.

Goldstein, Paul. *Intellectual Property: The Tough New Realities That Could Make or Break Your Business*. New York: Portfolio, 2007.

Gollin, Michael A. *Driving Innovation: Intellectual Property Strategies for a Dynamic World*. Cambridge: Cambridge University Press, 2008.

Heller, Michael. *The Gridlock Economy*. New York: Basic Books, 2008. Companion Web site, http://www.gridlockeconomy.com.

Howe, Jeff. *Crowdsourcing: Why the Power of the Crowd Is Driving the Future of Business*. New York: Random House, 2008.

Iansiti, Marco, and Roy Levien. *The Keystone Advantage: What the New Dynamics of Business Ecosystems Mean for Strategy, Innovation, and Sustainability*. Cambridge, MA: Harvard Business School Press, 2004.

Lee, Jessie C. Y., ed. *IP Client Strategies in Asia: Leading Lawyers on Understanding Variations in Asian Intellectual Property Law Systems, Advocating for Improved Enforcement Practices, and Staying on Top of Local Patent Law Amendments*. Boston: Aspatore Books, 2009.

Lyrio, Alexandre, ed. *IP Client Strategies in Central and South America: Leading Lawyers on Building Client Relationships, Understanding the Impact of Recent Cases and Developments, and Recognizing Regional Influences on Intellectual Property Law*. Boston: Aspatore Books, 2009.

Lessig, Lawrence. *The Future of Ideas*. New York: Random House, 2001.

Li, Charlene, and Michael Bernhoff. *Groundswell: Winning in a World Transformed by Social Technologies*. Cambridge, MA: Harvard Business Press, 2008.

Malackowski, James, and Courtney Smith. *Intellectual Property and Financial Markets: A Valuation and Commercialization Handbook*. Hoboken, NJ: Wiley, 2009.

Palfrey, John, and Urs Gasser. *Born Digital: Understanding the First Generation of Digital Natives*. New York: Basic Books, 2008.

Penalver, Eduardo Moises, and Sonia K. Katyal. *Property Outlaws: How Squatters, Pirates, and Protestors Improve the Law of Ownership*. New Haven, CT: Yale University Press, 2010.

Phelps, Marshall, and David Kline. *Burning the Ships: Intellectual Property and the Transformation of Microsoft*. Hoboken, NJ: Wiley, 2009.

Raugust, Karen. *The Licensing Business Handbook*. 7th ed. New York: EPM Communications, 2008.

Razgaitis, Richard. *Valuation and Dealmaking of Technology-Based Intellectual Property: Principles, Methods, and Tools*. Hoboken, NJ: Wiley, 2009.

Redman, Thomas C. *Data Driven: Profiting from Your Most Important Business Asset*. Cambridge, MA: Harvard Business Press, 2008.

Rivette, Kevin G., and David Kline. *Rembrandts in the Attic: Unlocking the Hidden Value of Patents*. Cambridge, MA: Harvard Business Press, 2000.

Rogers, Thomas, and Andrew Szamosszegi. *Fair Use in the U.S. Economy: Economic Contribution of Industries Relying on Fair Use*. Washington, DC: Computer and Communications Industry Association, 2010. Available at http://www .ccianet.org.

Smith, Gordon V. *Intellectual Property: Licensing and Joint Venture Profit Strategies*. Hoboken, NJ: Wiley, 1998.

Von Hippel, Eric. *Democratizing Innovation*. Cambridge, MA: MIT Press, 2005.

Zittrain, Jonathan L. *The Future of the Internet—and How to Stop It*. New Haven, CT: Yale University Press, 2008.

Case Studies

Casadesus-Masanell, Ramon, Andres Hervas, and Jordan Mitchell, "Peer-to-Peer File Sharing and the Market for Digital Information Goods." Cambridge, MA: Harvard Business School Publishing, March 30, 2010.

Mark, Ken, and Mary Crossan. "Apple Inc.: iPods and iTunes." Unpublished paper, University of Western Ontario, 2007.

Yoffe, David B., and Michael Slind. "Apple Inc. 2008." Cambridge, MA: Harvard Business School Publishing, September 8, 2008.

Blogs and Other Web Sites

America Society of Composers. "Authors and Publishers (ASCAP) Ace Title Search." http://www.ascap.com/ace/index.html.

Berkeley Center for Law and Technology. http://www.law.berkeley.edu/insti tutes/bclt.

Berkeley Digital Library SunSITE. http://ucblibrary3.berkeley.edu/Copyright.

Berkman Center for Internet and Society at Harvard University. http://cyber .law.harvard.edu.

Center for Intellectual Property and Copyright in the Digital Environment, University of Maryland University College. http://www.umuc.edu/distance /odell/cip/cip.shtml.

Center for the Study of the Public Domain, Duke Law School. http://www.law .duke.edu/cspd.

Coalition for Twenty-First-Century Patent Reform. http://www.patents matter.com.

Columbia University Copyright Advisory Office. http://copyright.columbia .edu/copyright.

Copyright and Fair Use, Stanford University Libraries. http://fairuse.stanford.edu.

Copyright Clearance Center. http://www.copyright.com.

Copyright Crash Course, University of Texas. http://www.utsystem.edu/OGC /IntellectualProperty/cprtindx.htm.

Cornell Legal Information Institute. "Copyright." http://topics.law.cornell.edu /wex/Copyright

Creative Commons. http://creativecommons.org.

Electronic Frontier Foundation. http://www.eff.org.

ExclusiveRights. http://www.exclusiverights.net.

Gassoway, Lolly. "When Works Pass into the Public Domain" (chart). University of North Carolina at Chapel Hill. http://www.unc.edu/~unclng/public-d.htm.

Guide to the Licensing World. http://www.licensingworld.co.uk.

IP Mall, Pierce Law Center. http://www.ipmall.info.

Kernochan Center for Law Media and the Arts, Columbia Law School. http://kernochancenter.org.

Patently-O. http://patentlaw.typepad.com.

Recording Industry Association of America. http://www.riaa.com.

Stanford IP Litigation Clearinghouse. http://www.law.stanford.edu/program/centers/iplc/#overview.

Stanford Law School Center for Internet and Society. http://cyberlaw.stanford.edu.

US Patent and Trademark Office. http://www.uspto.gov.

World Intellectual Property Organization. http://www.wipo.int.

World Trade Organization. "Intellectual Property Rights." http://www.wto.org/english/tratop_E/trips_e/trips_e.htm.

ABOUT THE AUTHOR

John Palfrey is the Henry N. Ess III Professor of Law as well as vice dean for library and information resources at Harvard Law School. He is also faculty codirector of the Berkman Center for Internet and Society at Harvard University (http://cyber.law.harvard.edu), and a venture executive at Highland Capital Partners (http://www.hcp.com). His research and teaching focus on the impact of the Internet on businesses, the economy, and public policy. Palfrey cofounded several technology start-ups. Among other books, he is coauthor, with Urs Gasser, of *Born Digital: Understanding the First Generation of Digital Natives* (Basic Books, 2008). Along with Jonathan Zittrain and William Fisher, he coauthored an amicus brief to the US Supreme Court in the copyright law case *MGM v. Grokster*. He practiced intellectual property and corporate law at the leading international law firm of Ropes & Gray. Palfrey writes a blog (http://blogs.law.harvard.edu/palfrey) and on Twitter (@jpalfrey).

INDEX

JOHN PALFREY is Head of School at Phillips Academy, Andover, coauthor of *Born Digital: How Children Grow Up in a Digital Age*, and author of *Safe Spaces, Brave Spaces: Diversity and Free Expression in Education* (MIT Press).